Tractatus Politico-Philosophicus

"Our time is the age of postmodernity and of the clash of epochs. But a new age of humanity is rising. It is *evolutionity* or the evolutionary epoch which replaces modernity and postmodernity."

Tractatus Politico-Philosophicus (*Political-Philosophical Treatise*) aims to establish the principles of good governance and of a happy society, and to open up new directions for the future development of humankind. W. Julian Korab-Karpowicz demonstrates the necessity of, and provides a guide for, the redirection of humanity. He argues that this paradigm shift must involve changing the character of social life and politics from competitive to cooperative, encouraging moral and intellectual virtues, providing foundations for happy societies, promoting peace among countries, and building a strong international community.

W. Julian Korab-Karpowicz is a philosopher, political thinker, and professor at Zayed University in Dubai and Lazarski University in Warsaw. He received his doctorate at the University of Oxford. In the early 1980s, he was a student leader in Poland's Solidarity movement, and was then awarded a scholarship of the Leadership Development Office of the Presbyterian Church, USA. He is the author of five books, including *On the History of Political Philosophy* (Routledge, 2016).

T0383680

"The *Tractatus* is a remarkable and illuminating book that should be widely read. It discusses a number of important ideas that can contribute to the betterment and positive evolution of humanity."
—Professor Wendell O'Brien, *Morehead State University, USA*

"This thoughtful book is a guide for anyone inquiring about a positive world change. The contents are organized so that they're easy to recognize and assimilate. I am truly impressed by the book."
—Professor William Auden,
Western Connecticut State University, USA

"The book is one of the most distinguishing titles in political philosophy that I have read in the last few years. It is equally important for academicians, political activists and lovers of human dignity. Korab-Karpowicz has boldly gone to the heart of our today's concerns and opened up a contemporary discourse to the exciting possibility of human evolution."
—Professor Dilipkumar Mohanta, *University of Calcutta, India*

Tractatus Politico-Philosophicus

New Directions for the Future
Development of Humankind

W. Julian Korab-Karpowicz

Routledge
Taylor & Francis Group

LONDON AND NEW YORK

First published 2017
by Routledge

2 Park Square, Milton Park, Abingdon, Oxfordshire OX14 4RN
52 Vanderbilt Avenue, New York, NY 10017

Routledge is an imprint of the Taylor & Francis Group, an informa business

First issued in paperback 2019

Library of Congress Cataloging-in-Publication Data
A catalog record for this book has been requested

ISBN: 978-1-138-06641-0 (hbk)
ISBN: 978-0-367-88890-9 (pbk)

Typeset in Times New Roman
by Apex CoVantage, LLC

This book is dedicated to Dr. David Hayes.

No man ever achieves anything, new or old, fundamental or peripheral, sound or fantastic, through his own unaided efforts.

Bronislaw Malinowski

Contents

Preface

Almost one hundred years have passed since Ludwig Wittgenstein wrote his *Tractatus Logico-Philosophicus*. In this book, Wittgenstein reduced the world to a set of facts and removed values from it. In a world that is the totality of facts, there can be no ethical propositions, ethics cannot be expressed, and there can be no philosophical reflection on a good life.

Over the past hundred years, humankind has survived two world wars, the massive tragedy that was the Holocaust, and many other cruel events that resulted in the destruction of entire cultures and nations. A distinctive feature of this period is the presence of ideologies, from left to right wing. It seems that in spite of the significant technological advancement that has occurred in the last hundred years, humanity has undergone an ideological enslavement and lost the ability to think independently and rationally about politics.

My book attempts to prove that the world created by human beings is primarily a world of values, and that ethics and political thinking are possible. I present a vision of the good state and a happy society. I show that the main value of social life and the basis of politics is cooperation. Like Wittgenstein, I use numbering to designate the issues discussed, and the sections numbered 7 to 7.54 are my responses to the propositions included in his sections 7 and 6.4 to 6.54.

As a philosophical work, my book is motivated by the search for truth. However, I am not of the opinion that the truth of the thoughts communicated here is unassailable and definitive. An "unassailable and definitive" truth is usually a dogma, and dogma is the basis of ideology, not philosophy. Rather than presenting the final clarification of all problems, my book instead indicates a new direction for humanity to take in order to complete its task and reach happiness: the way of cooperation and conscious evolution.

W. Julian Korab-Karpowicz

Acknowledgments

Two years after the publication of *Tractatus Politico-Philosophicus* by Derewiecki in Poland as a bilingual Polish/English edition, the English version of the *Tractatus* is published by Routledge in the United States. I have also added an introduction to the new edition. I have also made minor changes in the text and some corrections in numbering.

I would like to thank Natalja Mortensen, Political Editor at Routledge, and her colleagues for preparing the publication of my book. I am also very grateful to my reviewers for their helpful comments and generous opinions. In addition, I want to express my gratitude to Robert Turner for proofreading and my deep appreciation to professors Edward Niewiadomski and Adam Olech for their insights, advice, and encouragement. Finally, I wish to thank Zayed University for supporting the completion of the *Tractatus* by a research grant.

Introduction

Tractatus Politico-Philosophicus (*Political-Philosophical Treatise*) aims to establish the principles of good governance and of a happy society, and to open up new directions for the future development of humankind. In an age that has so often declared the end of philosophy, a philosophical treatise on politics may be received with surprise. Therefore, in this introduction, I will try to show that philosophy is still a viable enterprise. To prove my thesis and provide the background of my work, I shall discuss human evolution, refer to the new science, describe the new politics, as I envision it, and explain my methodology.

On Human Evolution

One of the most powerful and comprehensive philosophical ideas is that of human evolution. It has been discussed by Teilhard de Chardin, Julian Huxley,[1] and other thinkers,[2] and is linked to the evolutionary view of reality. The concept of evolution, the idea that reality or what-exists emerges in phases, cosmic, biological and human, in a process that generates novelty, variety, and sophistication, does not need to be understood as challenging the creation view, namely, that the world was created by God. Evolution is a creative process. Divine creation can proceed by the way of evolution. Whether reality is created or originates by itself or has always existed, science cannot answer. What is existence? Why does the world exist? How did it come about? Was it created or did it originate by itself? What was there before? These questions belong to the Mystery of Existence and transcend the limits of human understanding. They are philosophical or theological questions that fall outside the scientific domain.

It is characteristic of human beings that they can subject their lives to self-reflection, create culture, purposively change their environment, and thus engage in conscious evolution. Human evolution is still to a degree biological, depending on gene selection and proper nutrition; but primarily it is cultural, based on transmission of knowledge and values. We are no longer subjected to the automatic agency of natural selection. We are not mechanically determined in any way. The character of our future existence largely depends on our consciously and purposely developed material, moral, and intellectual environment: on our prosperity, education, beliefs, ideals, and traditions. Variations in them are reflected in individual, ethnic, national, class, and religious differences. Further, we need to realize that outcomes of both cosmic and biological evolutions are essentially completed, and their results can be seen in the natural environment of Earth.[3] Perhaps among billions of celestial bodies in the universe we can find one that has equally good conditions for biological life as ours. However, because of the complexity of the evolutionary process, the probability of finding such a place is very low. Similarly, perhaps among countless planets we can find one that has creatures like human beings. However, again, because of the sophistication of our mental abilities, the probability of finding such a being is very low. Thus, it is very likely that we are the only beings in the whole universe who have the capacities to carry evolution on.

Josef Hoene-Wroński, a nineteenth-century mathematician and philosopher, described human evolution in four basic stages, which in my contemporary reading are as follows. First, as humanity emerges from barbarity, where there is no established moral order, the initial stage of human evolution comes with the great codes of law. These are the laws of Hammurabi in Babylon, of Moses in Israel, of Manu in India, and of other lawgivers in places where early civilizations started to develop. The task of these legal codes was to provide human beings with a basic moral guidance. Inspiring the fear of punishment, they tried to inspire obedience by acting on the threat of external force alone.[4] The second stage of evolution takes place in ancient Greece and Rome. Not only is political freedom then discovered and practically implemented in the Athenian polis, and later in the Roman republic, but also, with the beginning of philosophy, there is a development of free rational inquiry and of ethical thinking based on virtue. The ideas of virtuous conduct and of natural law then discovered refer to our inner moral qualities, and not to an external threat. Morality is further internalized in the third stage, which begins with Christianity. We cannot be forced to love others but can only internalize love in ourselves. The essential Christian ethical teachings are thus founded on our inner discipline and moral self-transformation. They introduce into our lives an element of spiritual freedom, which has creative and transforming influence on both our personal inner experiences and on the historical destiny of our societies. They produce an essential social dynamism, which causes that the changing of the world for better becomes an integral part of the Western ideal. Then, the fourth stage of evolution comes with modernity, which represents progress, but at the same time a decline. Modernity, grounded in the idea of a positive self-transformation, adopts the idea of progress as one of its leading ideas. However, it understands it in a narrow sense as a scientific progress and the improvement of material conditions of life, while it dismisses religion and its moral teachings. Ethics becomes increasingly removed from politics in both theory and social practice. Thus, while making so many wonderful scientific and technological advancements, modern humankind experiences at the same time numerous social problems, revolutions, and wars. Because our vast technological powers have been separated from morality and even partially from rationality, there is a real danger that humanity will retreat to the first stage of its evolution, or even to barbarity.

When in the early nineteenth century he wrote his *Messianisme*, Hoene-Wroński did not have the abundance of sources of information about different civilizations that we have today. Thus, his views may sound rather Eurocentric. Certainly, we can enrich his picture by tracing the evolution of moral concepts and their impact on societies in India, China, and in the Muslim world.[5] These developments do not need to be parallel to each other because each civilization depends on its own traditions and values, and develops at its own pace. Nevertheless, his observation that in addition to the lust for power and wealth, which is so evident in European history, we can also find in the West the transforming intellectual and moral dynamics, which have contributed to a positive social and technological world change, is worth considering, as well as his conclusions.

The next, fifth stage of human evolution, which is not yet completed, but which he believed had already begun during his times, is the age of revolutionary changes and severe conflicts. All sorts of potentially conflicting issues that divide humanity are there: religious, economic, political, civilizational; and they are often presented in a rigid, dogmatic form and defended furiously by opposing camps. As a result, there is excessive violence, largely ideologically motivated. Everyone fights everyone, not just for power or for wealth, but for beliefs and particularly for the ultimate superiority of one's own belief. This is the current stage of the most scientifically and technologically developed humankind. It comes with the forgetfulness of who we really are, weakening of our religion, and the erosion of our morals. The consequences of these are major world wars and numerous smaller conflicts. Is there a way out? Like de Chardin and Huxley, Hoene-Wroński believes that, first of all, we need to recognize our true human identity and our destiny as humankind. Power is not the proper goal. The true end is not for any particular nation, religion, ideology, or political or economic system to overcome all the rest and affirm its unchallenged world domination. We have a higher task to be completed. We are vehicles of further evolution. In this phase evolution is no longer related merely to matter, but proceeds through the development of mind, as it is expressed in our scientific and technological achievements. However, the expansion of knowledge aimed at our intellectual perfection is not enough, if ethics is lacking. To bring "absolute Truth" and "absolute Goodness" together, as Hoene-Wroński writes—or in my words, to pursue both intellectual and moral perfection, by the way of self-transformation—is to put humanity on the right track again. The precondition for this is, as I advise in this *Tractatus*, to depart from a world turn apart by conflict and proceed by the way of cooperation.

Julian Huxley, whose ideas on human evolution, presented in *Evolutionary Humanism*, are very inspiring, made one serious mistake. He tried to replace traditional religions with his new religion of humanism.[6] Other secular humanists go even further in their attempt to remove divinity and religion completely from the world. However, if we really want to proceed further with evolution, as Huxley certainly desired, we cannot alienate large groups of people—in this particular case, those who believe in God—and create divisions among humankind that can lead to fervent conflicts. It is impossible to cooperate always with everyone; however, as a general rule, human progress can be achieved only if we work cooperatively together. "Cooperation is based on the issues that unite people, as opposed to those that divide them" (1.52).[7] It can be achieved on the basis of the needs and beliefs that we can share in common. Therefore, we cannot disregard people's religious sensitivities and declare that we now want to remove something that they regard as most important for their lives. Further, we can possibly develop successfully a new science or a new philosophy, for these enterprises can be planned and involve rational inquiry; but we cannot create by will any new religion because religion is not just a domain of rationality, but a domain of feelings and is usually a product of extraordinary vision and inspiration. Hence, the project of a new, humanist religion, based on reason alone, can never succeed and can only be regarded as a utopia.

Huxley wanted to construct a new secular religion because he believed that traditional religions involve negative aspects, such as dogmas and superstitions. This observation is correct, mainly if we consider religions at a popular level. However, we can note that secular ideologies are also not free from dogmas. These are results of our limited understanding of complex phenomena and our tendency to simplify them. Dogmas and superstitions are then not only a religious issue but also an ideological one, and are related to inherent limitations of the human mind. Further, like other secular humanists, Huxley overlooks a positive aspect of traditional religion; it is its moral teaching. On the positive side, religion "shapes the character of human beings, influences their moral education, builds their community of values, produces solidarity among them, and fills their minds with a higher content than do the things of everyday life" (3.822). It develops us morally and protects us from demoralization. Consequently, human evolution cannot advance by alienating traditional religions. On the contrary, it requires including them in the evolutionary process and directing them wisely to the source of their own spirituality. At the deep, spiritual level of religion, which is a moral level, humanity can find a common ground. It can proceed beyond superficial religious and civilizational barriers, and come to mutual understanding and peace. "In today's situation of large-scale manipulation and escalating conflict in the world, the peace that humanity desperately needs should begin as peace among religions" (7.632). Thus, instead of attempting to weaken or even to destroy religions, we should rather invite them all to participate in the moral and intellectual development of humankind.

There is one fundamental objection against human evolution that is stressed by some theologians and political scientists in the West. They claim that, because of their nature, human beings cannot be morally improved. For Reinhold Niebuhr the "idea that humankind can perfect itself by its own efforts . . . is the essence of sinfulness and the refusal to acknowledge human finiteness."[8] Niebuhr's theological belief in original sin and the incurable corruption of human beings, at least in this world, is echoed by Hans Morgenthau's description of human beings as essentially power driven and egoistic,[9] and by the beliefs of other international relations scholars that wars, even if we recognize them as being extremely destructive and morally ugly, will occur again and again, and that there will never be a truly lasting peace.[10]

In response, I would argue that the opinions provided above are metaphysical visions of some sort. They potentially construct our reality rather than provide its factual descriptions. Certainly, we as human beings have capacities to do both evil and good. This can be proven by countless examples. However, whether we treat our neighbor with love or hatred or whether there should be war or peace largely depends on our own choices. As many Christian theologians say, to perfect ourselves by our own efforts may not be enough, and we might need God's grace. But more importantly, in Christianity the possibility of human perfection is acknowledged in Christ's saying: "Be perfect, therefore, even as your heavenly Father is perfect" (Matt. 5:48). Our moral imperfection can eventually be overcome by faith and love. Human moral perfectibility is also recognized in Islam. Muslims believe that although human beings have an inclination to err, they can also recognize goodness. *Falah* (success) in building a moral order depends on our submission to Qur'anic guidance.[11] Then, in Indian thought, our perfectibility is not only possible, but constitutes the essence of human life. Hindus and Buddhists believe that each of us will have to be reborn, unable to escape the circle of life and death, until his or her personal perfection is realized. To conclude: "Human nature is unalterable" (2) and "cannot be transformed by any revolutionary change" (2.1). This is not because we are permanently either good or bad, but because we are evolutionary beings, capable of self-transformation and of moral and intellectual improvement, and to perfect ourselves and carry on evolution is our destiny.

Our biological evolution was basically completed several thousand years ago. Since then human bodies and brains have remained structurally the same. However, this does not mean that we are complete. Future technologies can improve our bodies. Moreover, we have already moved from biological to cultural evolution. This has been proved by so many wonderful human achievements, the results of the development of conceptual thought and symbolic language. Last but not least, the case of human evolution, particularly its intellectual side, is strongly supported today by the development of the new science: by its fresh, hitherto unthought-of, ground breaking discoveries and the novel perspectives that it opens for humankind.

On the New Science

According to the classical, Newtonian science, the natural world is deterministic and predictable. This picture has in turn determined how human phenomena are studied. Beginning with Thomas Hobbes[12]— who, following the scientific model of his epoch, wanted to make political science as precise as geometry, considered the universe as nothing but body in motion, and studied phenomena by applying the reductionist method—social scientists have tried to describe human beings as if they were bundles of appetites and aversions, to make them into living machines, to reduce complex social phenomena to their parts, and to subject politics to deterministic laws. But in the meantime physics has changed. It has discovered that at the subatomic level determinism no longer applies and the character of occurrences is probabilistic. Today's physicists no longer try to reduce all aspects of phenomena to the interactions of their smallest constituents, but rather stress their relationships, and particularly the relations with their environment. The universe is no longer considered as a machine, but rather as a dynamic whole, whose parts are interrelated. Moreover, the Cartesian division between mind and matter has been challenged. It has been discovered that the mind of the observer is not only necessary to observe things, but also to bring about their properties. However, perhaps the greatest challenge that the new science presents to the older worldview is related to the context of discovery. It questions the standard empiricist or positivistic position that no substantial thesis about the world can be accepted in science independently of observation and experiment. It shows that we cannot separate scientific inquiry from philosophical assumptions, and that it is philosophical, intuitive thinking that is essential for the expansion of knowledge.

The achievements of today's science are astonishing. Scientific knowledge continues to grow rapidly and subjects to its research new domains of phenomena, creating as a result new disciplines such as cosmology or molecular biology. In addition, science continues to stimulate the advancement of new technologies. It is very successful both in the development of its theoretical concepts and in the wealth of its practical applications. However, scientific progress is not merely a result of meritorious studies of phenomena based on evidence and accumulation of empirical data. It depends on the acceptance of new ideas about the universe, which help to comprehend and describe it better than rival views. The success of science, as Nicholas Maxwell eloquently argues, is due to the progressive adoption of new metaphysical visions that describe the universe better than earlier views, and of methods and theories appropriate to these new visions. These visions or ideas of the universe are "assumptions concerning [its] comprehensibility and knowability."[13] Their progressive adoption does not refer only to the replacement of concepts based on Aristotelian metaphysics by those of Newtonian mechanics and then by those of Einstein's space-time and by those of quantum mechanics. Within the framework of modern physics, we can witness a continuous innovation. If we consider, for example, the scientific picture of fundamental physical entities, in Maxwell's description, they have been believed to be, in turn:

> small, rigid corpuscles that interact only by contact; point-particles that interact at a distance; a rigid quasimaterialistic stuff spread throughout the universe (the ether); a continuously varied field spread throughout the space within which point-particles are embedded; a self-interacting field; curved space-time, probabilistic quantum objects; quantum fields; superstrings.[14]

These views of physical entities are not unrelated, but actually they represent more and more complete and accurate approximations to the nature of physical reality. New philosophical ideas or metaphysical visions that replace the old ones, extend or improve earlier approximations. They try to unveil the subsequent layers of reality itself.

What is reality? In a narrow positivistic or empirical vision, whose expression can be found in Wittgenstein's *Tractatus Logico-Philosophicus*, facts are the whole reality. He declares: "The world is the totality of facts" and "The world divides into facts." "The whole reality is the world."[15] These declarations can serve as an example of how positivism, which declares itself an antimetaphysical program, formulates a metaphysical thesis and at the same time is unaware of it.[16] For the positivists, to exist is to be perceived. Reality, what exists, is sensible facts, denoting what can be observed. These depend on sensory perceptions of the observer. Statements about them, based on observation and experiment, are meant to be objective. They are assumed to be independent of any subjective conditions related to observations. The assumption is that we can distinguish between object and subject, and observe objects without influencing them. Thus, in the positivist worldview, one of the key characteristics of science is objectivity. Values and other qualitative attributes of the world that cannot be observed and classified as facts are considered the domain of subjectivity, the matter of personal preference, and as such are excluded from reality and scientific inquiry. Statements about them are denied any sense. This is why for Wittgenstein, as well as for other positivists, ethics, a domain of values, cannot be meaningfully expressed. Positivism in social sciences excludes the possibility of a rational, theoretical discussion of a morally and politically good life, and of making meaningful value choices. But as one of the leading exponents of the new physics, Fritjof Capra, claims, by transcending the Cartesian division between body and mind, the new science "has not only invalidated the classical ideal of objective description of nature but has also challenged the myth of value-free science."[17] There is always subjectivity in objectivity. While it is not apparent in classical physics, which, as Heisenberg describes, "can be considered as that idealization in which we speak about the world as completely separated from ourselves,"[18] it becomes evident at the subatomic level, investigated in quantum theory, where the observed electrons do not have properties independent from the mind of the observer. Hence, positivism conceals an implicit subjectivism that is present in the cognitive process. It does not understand that its description of reality as facts is only an interpretation, but takes facts to be reality itself and derives from this view practical consequences related to the possibility of thinking and speaking meaningfully about values.

Values can be defined as the "qualities that human beings appreciate because of their usefulness or their role in the satisfaction of human needs" (2.555). If we agree with the positivists that values cannot be known by direct observation such as physical phenomena, this does not mean that values cannot be known at all, or do not exist, or are merely subjective. Since in knowing the world, our subjectivity is always involved—or there is always a knower and what is to be known—facts are essentially subjective. However, just as it is possible to communicate facts to others and agree on statements concerning them, because if we practice impartiality and neutrality, they can be made inter-subjective, and in this sense, also objective, so also it is possible to express values with sense, agree on them, and implement them in our lives. Hence, rationality and meaningfulness are not merely limited to factuality. We can speak rationally and meaningfully about values as well. Further, only human beings can think and act in terms of values. They are the essential part of our human reality. To disregard them as lacking sense would impoverish reality itself, remove one of its important dimensions. In so far as human reality is concerned, the world is "something more than the totality of facts, and propositions can express something higher than facts" (7.202). "The world is the totality of values, rather than the totality of facts" (7.2021). Compared to the world as the totality of facts, the world as the totality of values is like the quantum world compared to the world of classical physics. While the latter is deterministic and can be described by causal laws, the former presupposes uncertainty and creativity. The world that human beings create, the human-made environment, "is a result of the values they adopt" (7.8). "What is our goal?" (7.71) "What will we pass on to future generations?" (7.73) In order to answer these questions, findings of science are not sufficient. Even the most advanced science remains only a partial knowledge about some part of reality; but we are asking here about the whole of reality in which we, humans, are included. Therefore, we need to engage in a philosophical reflection. Our answers will depend on the state of our current knowledge, including self-knowledge, or on the state of our consciousness. Consciousness, and particularly its states or levels, is thus another dimension of reality.

New theories, especially quantum theory, have shown that our reality, even the physical one, is far more complex than we had earlier imagined. They have brought important revisions of our earlier conceptions of the universe and our relations to it. They depict a more sophisticated natural environment than that which can be described by the notions of objectivity and of cause and effect. Elementary particles observed by quantum scientists appear in a network of interactions. They also develop a relationship to the observer, leading us to the conclusion that at a deeper level of reality, we cannot study anything as separate from ourselves. Thus the ideal of scientific objectivity, as an object standing over and against the subject, disappears. Further, our acts of observation and of theorizing about reality are a part of the process that brings it forth. Reality is thus not merely a set of facts arrested in a process observation. It does not have a static quality, but a dynamic one. It is modified according to our engagement with it. This idea applies not only to the subatomic level, but also to social life. The dynamism of human relationships is expressed in values that we learn and adopt. Our relationship can be loving, indifferent, or hateful. It can be also friendly, respectful, and tolerant, or characterized by their opposites. Because of different values that we apply to them, social relationships allow for a great dynamism and are far more complex than those that we encounter in quantum mechanics. They cannot be easily calculated even by most complicated mathematical equations. Nevertheless, they share many similarities.

There is now growing interest in applying the discoveries of the new science to social sciences. The evidence for this could be, for example, the recent excellent work of Alexander Wendt, *Quantum Mind and Social Science*. However, as Werner Heisenberg, a Nobel Prize-winning physicist who is known for the development of quantum theory, noted some time ago, we should not apply forcefully "scientific concepts in domains where they do not belong."[19] It is rather mistaken to believe that we can build a social science with the help of formal models used in quantum theory and calculate utilities by using new formulas. To do so would be an attempt to interpret discoveries of the new science in the spirit of an outdated early modern philosophy. It is true that human beings cannot violate the laws of physics, as Wendt argues, but it is equally true that the laws of physics cannot fully describe human behavior.[20] Therefore, instead of trying to relate new scientific theories directly to social phenomena, we should let them help us to overcome the narrow empiricist and materialistic interpretations of reality derived from Newtonian physics that still largely prevail over our minds. As these theories cogently explain, the world represents a system of coherent, evolving, interactive processes that only temporarily manifest themselves as stable structures. Its infinite complexity and ever-growing diversity can be only artificially arrested by control and reduced to uniformity. These insights derived from the new science should guide us to a new vision of politics that would be less based on fragmentation and division, as exemplified in modern individualism, but more connecting and holistic, and thus more appropriate to our new evolutionary epoch.

On the New Politics

As has been shown above, objectivity cannot be separated from subjectivity. If we can speak rationally and meaningfully about facts, we can also speak rationally and meaningfully about values. If statements concerning values could not be expressed with sense, as positivists claim, and were merely a matter of personal preference, we could not meaningfully discuss political ideas, such as freedom or justice. Statements about them would then become merely something related to an individual or group choice, and assume the forms of different ideologies. We could not reasonably decide then which of these ideologies is true, and they would become like those incommensurable paradigms that cannot be measured against one another, but can only be eventually tolerated. However, since we cannot rely merely on the celebration of plurality, but also need to choose certain values and ideological frameworks to guide our lives, our choice would finally depend not on reason, but on power. Whether or not it is made explicit in the positivist program, once the possibility of rational discussion and meaningful evaluation of something is removed, then power becomes what really counts in our societies at both theoretical and practical levels. It decides about values, defines them, and like in Hobbes and his followers, constitutes the highest value itself. Thus, under the influence of positivism and other modern doctrines, will to power and desire to control become the leading features of modernity. This translates in practice into the untamed human conquest of nature, conflict-riven societies, recurrent destructive wars, and the conflicting character of international relations. Politics is theoretically defined as a struggle for power, with the exclusion of other views, and this is also what it becomes in social practice. It is difficult to find a better illustration of the profound, yet mostly unreflected-upon influence of philosophical ideas on human life.

Human reality is principally self-created. The force of creation belongs to our ideas and not to our material conditions, which can merely influence our thinking to some degree. By discovering new ideas in physics, we can better understand physical reality, but we cannot change it; by discovering new ideas in philosophy or politics, we can not only understand but also change human reality. We cannot alter the laws of physics; but we can alter the laws by which we are guided. "It belongs to the nature of the human being to be able to create culture" (2.54). By creating culture—our artificial environment (material, social, spiritual)—we transcend the limitations associated with our original, natural animal endowment. We proceed beyond mere obedience to biological drives and discover freedom, the possibility of self-realization. We can thus self-create and transform ourselves. Our reality is our culture or the environment that we create. "The development of culture knows no boundaries" (2.553). But culture can be adopted and developed for both constructive and destructive goals. We have the ability to build and to destroy. "Slavery and war are the results of the development of culture, just as are science and art" (2.5421). Therefore, what we will make of our lives largely depends on our choice, particularly on the choice of values that guide our lives, and our right choice depends on our correct recognition of whom we really are. "We were not born here on Earth to become consumers or militants" (7.76), nor to merely to seek wealth and power, but to fully develop morally and intellectually. Power, ability to do something, can only be a means, never the goal, which is our perfectibility. Within the universe as we know it, we represent the pinnacle of evolution. This is reflected in our ability to think, invent things, and plan ahead, and in our capacity for ethical thought. However, we are not yet complete beings. At present, there is a huge difference between the development of our scientific knowledge and technological abilities, and our moral growth. Morality and rationality are dynamic phenomena; they cannot be prescribed by unchanging rules, but have to be internalized. We can still further develop in ourselves our moral sensitivity and intellectual curiosity. We may include in the basic imperative "do not harm" not only our fellow human beings, but also the animal world and even the natural world at large. We can enlarge our understanding of the place and role of human beings in the universe and our ecological awareness. At this stage, human evolution becomes a conscious evolution, a self-transforming process.

It is an enormous task, which requires that human beings cooperate with each other for its completion.

The new politics is based on the awareness of human identity and on the role of human beings in the evolutionary process. With the new politics, a new age of humanity begins. It is the evolutionary epoch that replaces modernity and postmodernity. While modernity was inspired by the mechanistic, materialistic, and deterministic view of the universe emerging from Newtonian physics and tried to apply this view to living organisms and social phenomena, and postmodernity has been characterized by unsolved problems related to globalization, political instability, and a regress to irrationality, the evolutionary epoch or *evolutionity* is inspired by the idea of human evolution, and by the organic and holistic worldview emerging from the new science. It is not revolutionary, like most modern and post-modern intellectual and political movements, but evolutionary. It is not against traditions, but rather appreciates their value and tries to build on them. It does not want to undermine religions, but rather seeks to uncover what is truly valuable in them—their spirituality. Particularly, it revitalizes the tradition of classical rationality. "In classical rationality, reasoning is not only an instrument to achieve various benefits, but primarily an axiological reflection on what is morally good or bad, favorable or unfavorable, right or wrong" (9.212). Classical rationality, which at its core is an evolutionary one, involves thinking and speaking meaningfully about values. It is expressed in politics "in the pragmatism of actions aimed at a good life" (9.216). A good life is not only "the wealth or material prosper-ity of human beings, but also their spiritual (moral and intellectual) development" (1.21). It leads to their happiness or self-realization.

To consider happiness as a normative goal of society and the state is an old tradition that goes back to Aristotle and his notion of *eudai-monia*.[21] However, *Tractatus Politico-Philosophicus* is not merely an Aristotelian or classical project, but one that is inspired by and advances human evolution. I agree with Aristotle that happiness is more than a passing moment of joy and signifies our flourishing or fulfilling life, our self-realization, the highest good that human beings usually desire. It is difficult to imagine that anyone would like to be unhappy, i.e., would not like to prosper materially and to develop mentally, and if we find such a case, it would be a strange one indeed. Further, I agree with Aristotle that while happiness is related to satisfying our various needs, it cannot be reduced to sensual pleasure, nor to the satisfaction of endless desires, as Hobbes famously claimed. Nevertheless, contrary to Aristotle, I do not endorse any special lifestyle, such as the contemplative, and do not promote a particular concept of happiness related to it. My basic assumption is that all human beings have the same nature, the same basic desires and needs, and "the same goal, which is happiness" (2.5351). But because of their different social and cultural backgrounds, and their individual personalities, they can individually modify their needs and restrain their desires, and understand happiness or self-realization in various ways. "A society is a diverse community. It consists of people who differ from each other in their level of affluence, intelligence, and education, as well as their character traits" (3.211). What is important to all of us is a sense of achievement, a fulfilling life, which is expressed in the word "self-realization." Some people might find self-realization or fulfillment in the theoretical life of a scientist, others in the active life of a politician or a business person, still others in an undistinguished life of everyday activities and of many simple pleasures; finally, many may find their self-realization in spiritual pursuits and a search for eternal happiness. What would be an advancement for some of us could be a failure for others. Further, as our societies develop in terms of their organization and sophistication, what most people understand by happiness can change. Consequently, we cannot mechanically prescribe the same notion of happiness or self-realization to everyone. "A happy society is one in which everyone has an opportunity for self-realization and respects the self-realization of others" (10.03). In a happy society, we pursue happiness, as we best understand it ourselves, yet without imposing it forcefully on others or obtaining it at the cost to others. Lastly, since we are all moral and rational beings, our self-realization "is expressed most fully in moral and intellectual perfection" (2.5352).

Moral and intellectual perfection cannot be imposed on human beings from above. It can only be internalized and considered as the ultimate goal toward which we strive. Only at an early stage of human evolution can morality be forcefully imposed on people by unchanging laws. However, such an imposition does not guarantee any moral progress. It merely fixes human beings in one limited ethical model. Similarly, to request that people develop intellectually by following unchanging views of the world and stationary rules of reasoning would impede rather than stimulate their mental growth. To further develop mentally and become innovative, they need to discover intellectual curiosity in themselves, be allowed to challenge their earlier views, and be able to freely exercise their thinking.

Consequently, at later stages of human evolution, both the development of morality and the expansion of knowledge have to become internal processes. This internality is expressed in the idea of moral and intellectual virtues, particularly in the highest ones: love and wisdom. As people become virtuous, they discover an inner joy in doing things that are ethically right, just as they find an inner joy in discovering new things and expanding their knowledge. Those who find joy in virtuous or noble acts are properly speaking the nobility. Therefore, a happy society, even a democratic one, must always include a noble element. A good democracy is *sophocracy*, an ennobled democracy (6). It must be based on virtues. If virtues, particularly integrity and wisdom, are missing from politics, then it gets corrupted. It loses its essential character of good governance and becomes a mere play of different, mainly commercial, interests. It is dominated by powerful lobbies and is populated by mediocre individuals who usurp authority since they often lack moral and intellectual qualifications for leadership. Social life becomes then increasingly commercialized, split apart by conflicts, uncertain about the future, manipulated by media, and deprived of much place for the fine arts and for deeper philosophical or religious reflection. To resist these trends and to advance human evolution, there must be in society a moral and intellectual elite: the elite of honor and merit. It is "the minority group, comprising people who are noble, resourceful, and educated, that in every generation contributes to the maintenance and development of various aspects of culture" (6.731). If such people are lacking or are replaced by others who are less diligent and less talented, or who, lacking integrity, merely exploit others, by forming a so-called "parasitic elite" (6.662), our culture, and ultimately our civilization, declines.

The organic conception of the world, inspired by the new science, presupposes growth and what I describe as "the laws of liberty." They are "rules for successful action—action that brings benefits to the individual or group and is not associated with doing harm to other human beings" (4.21). These laws regard societies as organisms and develop them on the basis of peoples' traditions and experiences. The basic difference between machines (mechanisms) and organisms, as Capra rightly notes, is "that machines are constructed, whereas organisms grow."[22] The views of society and of the state that still dominate our textbooks go back to the Hobbesian and Lockean ideas of social contract. They refer to constructs or mechanisms. When Hobbes and Locke applied their concepts of human beings motivated by power and self-interest to social phenomena, they were guided by the intention to describe human behavior by laws similar to those that govern the Newtonian universe. They conveyed to us "a mechanical picture of the human being driven by desires" (2.554). But this cannot work. We are far too sophisticated to be described by the laws of physics. Our behavior cannot be merely explained by our desires, interests, or power-drives. We are not simple mechanisms "whose operation can be reduced to the pursuit of pleasure and the avoidance of suffering, or to selfishness and the struggle for power, but rather a complex organism of an axiological character" (2.5541). Only in some civilizations, namely in those that do not proceed beyond or decline to the first stage of human evolution, is there mechanization of humankind based on coercion. An example of such a civilization is the oriental-Byzantine civilization, or in short "Byzantism," which gradually "eliminates freedom by means of its all-powerful bureaucracy and its extended mechanism of control over all aspects of human existence" (5.43). It is my suggestion that to revitalize our Western civilization, we need to go beyond Byzantism and Militarism to the Classical Tradition or to our classical heritage: namely, away from domination, centralism, and uniformity to freedom, autonomy, and diversity. This is also what the new science suggests. If we want to describe human affairs, it is then better to use an organic analogy rather than to reduce them to a materialistic and mechanistic picture.

The fundamental principle of humankind is cooperation. We can perhaps imagine ourselves to be independent individuals or live in independent countries, but in fact we cannot achieve anything of importance without cooperation with others. Society is a diverse community linked by bonds of cooperation. It consists of people who differ from each other in their level of affluence, intelligence, and education, as well as their habits and character traits. They all need to work together to achieve individual and common goals. The idea of removing all differences, making all people alike, and arriving at a classless society is neither compatible with human nature nor conducive to human progress. Each social class or diverse social group represents some values and this is its potential contribution to the common good.

The basic values of the three basic classes which I consider the most important in society—labor, business, and honor—are freedom, entrepreneurship, and nobility (3.214). They all have their role in a happy society. Hence, instead of trying to make people or cultures the same, we shall recognize their unique differences based on their values and contributions. The greatest human advances in scientific discovery, creative art, and political leadership are usually due to remarkably gifted, exceptional individuals. Rather than being overwhelmingly concerned with equality, we should then pay more attention to quality. We must aim at increasing the quality of life. Our personalities, potentialities, and individualities constitute the world's greatest resources. Thus to move forward with human evolution, we need to cooperate to utilize our resources, work in a community, and yet retain our fruitful diversity. This applies not only to diversity based on values and contributions within societies, but also to the diversity of nation-states. They should not be replaced by a world state. Instead, they should act within the framework of an international community. The seven principles of political rationalism introduced in the *Tractatus* present a new vision of international politics. Our common task is to build a strong international community based on shared values and cooperation, with the goal of "advancing the prosperity, progress and perfection of all humanity" (9.51).

In this short introduction, only some ideas concerning the vision of the new politics can be mentioned. The *Tractatus* discusses a number of topics. To name just a few, these are: politics, human nature, the state, freedom, solidarity, democracy, civilization, family and marriage, power, international relations, war, and peace. Also, it introduces new words, such as *sophocracy*, ennobled democracy; *nativeculturalism*, an alternative to multiculturalism; or *parentsexuality*, a privileged form of sexuality. It addresses many issues that concern today's political thinkers. Some of the questions that I ask and try to answer are: What is a person? What is culture? What is civilization? What are the values of independent countries and local communities? What are the advantages and challenges related to living in multicultural societies? What is a happy society and what are its principles? How can we distinguish the morally and politically good from the bad? What relationship should human beings have to their environment? Can we find a basis for shared values that can bring us together as humankind? On what basis can the principles of global justice and solidarity be established? The main objective of my work is to demonstrate the necessity of, and provide a guide for, the redirection of humanity. I argue that this paradigm shift must involve changing the character of social life and politics from competitive to cooperative, encouraging moral and intellectual virtues, providing foundations for happy societies, promoting peace among countries, and building a strong international community. I try to show that the essence of politics is not a struggle for power, which can only be its derivative meaning, but rather the ability to organize society for cooperation and actualize a good life. Also, I try to remind humanity of its high task, which is moral and intellectual perfection, and the advancement of human evolution.

On My Method

Philosophy and science each have their methods proper to the problems that they want to solve. In each case methodology depends on epistemology and ontology. What are my ontological assumptions? I assume that reality is in a process of evolution and unfolds to us as we are ourselves engaged in a self-transforming, evolutionary process. In order to grasp the evolving reality, which is continually unfolding to us, our thinking itself must be evolutionary. It cannot be static, but must be dynamic. It must reject any dogmatic position, whether secular or religious, which tries to arrest change, to arrive at some limited and final ideological conclusions, and to see the end of human history in a definite form. Evolutionary thinking is based on a non-dogmatic, open-ended system of ideas that help us to comprehend the world in which we live, and direct our evolution.

In *Tractatus Politico-Philosophicus*, I propose a new idea-system. Ideas concerning different topics related to politics are introduced. From the main ideas others are deduced. Ideas are formulated thoughts. They are vehicles of knowledge. But since we change ourselves and our environment by ideas, by the way we think, they also create reality. Statements expressing ideas do not merely define social phenomena, but also describe them and often give them a purpose. However, proposing new ideas cannot be arbitrary. Inventing them is not merely exercising our fantasy. It must be guided by some reason and must attract the understanding of others and their support. This is the essence of the method of dialectic employed by Plato. What we come to believe is verified through discussion. Dialectic is a method by which we maintain an intellectual openness. It can assume a question-answer format, which is so characteristic of Platonic dialogues, or become internalized and become a form of rational thought.[23] It serves the triple purpose of clarification, verification, and discovery of knowledge. To justify themselves, ideas must be subjected to a logical, thoughtful, and practical test. To illustrate this, the first idea of my idea-system is expressed in the proposition: "Politics is the art of governing; it is essentially the organization of society for cooperation" (1). This proposition does not merely define politics, but also points to its essentially cooperative character. It does not involve any logical contradiction. If we subject the idea to a thoughtful and practical test, we can come to the conclusion that politics, as the art of governing whose purpose is to sustain cooperation in society, makes sense and is possible: it can be practically implemented. As it is clear from the proposition 1.15, this idea of politics disputes the influential idea that "all politics is a struggle for power." What is then the ontological difference between these two ideas and the idea-systems to which they belong? What are the two realities that come out of these two conceptions of politics? One is the reality of cooperation; one is the reality of conflict. Which one is more true? As the proposition 1.512 says, "if life were essentially conflict, then a world transformation would be impossible, there would be no progress, and nothing would ever grow." Conflict can be regarded as a part of life but not as its essence (1.1513). Consequently, while we can find examples of both cooperation and conflict in today's political life, the argument is that the idea of politics as the struggle for power represents a morally and ontologically impoverished picture of human reality.

As a social phenomenon, politics is obviously more complicated than the simple distinction between cooperation and conflict may suggest, and to illustrate its complexity, which involves moral, ideological, civilizational, and other factors, this whole book was written. However, what emerges from our initial consideration of the first idea is that different ideas lead us to different world-pictures. Again, to decide which of the pictures is more true, it is not enough to conduct empirical social research. The survey results are not yet sufficient to decide on what is really true. They tell us only about statistical occurrences and can eventually inform us whether something can occur or not, or what is more likely to occur. They are limited to facts, which are only one dimension of reality. They may be only factually true, but not axiologically and essentially true. In order to understand and to decide what is true to human beings, we must not only consider facts, but also values, and know what is essential to us. If we consider that we are evolutionary beings, creating culture, forming concepts and developing ideas, changing our environment, and thus self-creating ourselves, the picture of politics that is supportive of our nature and destiny would be more true to reality than a view of politics that is based merely on potentially erroneous factual evidence that is supported by a statistical majority.

Ideas that form an idea-system grow out of our thoughts and experiences. These represent worldviews, based on facts and values. What is the epistemological status of these ideas? They are holistic grasps of reality. These grasps are not direct research findings, such as quantitative results, but rather intuitive visions that may sometimes be inspired by them. Intuition is also a part of the method of dialectic. It operates on concepts and can consider their relationships in one glance. It discovers what is essential in phenomena. It belongs to our subjectivity, but it is not merely something subjective. It is based on what we already know: on what we have learned and observed. By contrast to analytic statements, which do not expand knowledge, but eventually infer conclusions from what is assumed or known, ideas based on intuitions are expressed in synthetic statements.

Synthetic, intuitive knowledge, which we find in philosophy and mathematics, is not merely a poetic imagination. It can be subjected to rational and empirical verification, of which the proof is the employment of mathematical ideas in today's physics.[24] Intuition can give us a vision. These visions or ideas, when applied in science, can move it forward. However, they can also be applied to other aspects of human life. If we study social phenomena by using research methods, we can eventually come to conclusions concerning how things are. But ideas that refer to holistic grasps of reality can tell us more. They can also advise how things can be and should be. Ultimately, ideas and concepts are the stepping stones of our evolution. Language is not merely a tool for communication, or a house of being; it is the creator of our reality. We create the world for ourselves by our language. By using a rich and beautiful language, we do not only increase our intelligence, but also our aesthetic and moral sensitivity. The role of our subjectivity is not merely, as Immanuel Kant discovered, to provide us with pure intuitions and categories, by which we can apprehend and know things as phenomena. We do not only know the world by means of concepts, but also are created by them—by all concepts that we form. As we form various concepts out of the raw material of our experience and they enter into our language, and are then used to form different ideas, they expand our knowledge and hence unveil reality. Obviously for some concepts such as "unicorn" or "phoenix" we do not find an empirical verification because they are only results of our imagination, but concepts describing values, such as courage, prudence, or freedom, refer to something real, and not merely subjective, for we can find expressions of these in the real world known to us, and can discuss ideas related to these concepts with others.

To conclude, philosophy, understood in a classical sense as a quest for complete knowledge of the whole, is possible, and we can speak meaningfully and rationally about values. Speaking about values, learning and internalizing them, develops us not only morally, but also intellectually, and expands the scope of our reality. But if we deny the possibility of expressing values and remove them from rational inquiry, we impoverish our world. The effect is that we then become demoralized, driven by will to power, rather than by will to achieve moral and intellectual perfection, which is our ultimate goal. In order to remind human beings of this goal and to move humanity in a right direction, I have written this *Tractatus*. It represents an idea-system. The ideas it presents are interconnected and there is some argumentation. The arguments in support of essential points and against some views are perhaps more implicit than plainly stated, but they become plain to careful readers who are acquainted with current issues and debates in political philosophy and international relations theory. Yet, to make the idea-system introduced in my work more universal, and thus longer lasting, opening up new directions for the future development of humankind, and not merely related to today's concerns, I have generally avoided direct references to contemporary affairs. The final words of the *Tractatus* are an allusion to Wittgenstein who, on the dedication page, quotes a motto that everything that can be known can be said in just three words. He does not say what these words are. I propose: "life, freedom, and cooperation" and conclude with the statement: "The purpose of the evolution of life is its fullness and perfection. Human evolution is a journey to ever greater freedom and to moral and intellectual perfection." This is my message to humanity.

Notes

1 See Julian Huxley, *Evolutionary Humanism*; Teilhard de Chardin, *The Phenomenon of Man*.
2 Among Indian philosophers who viewed human beings in an evolutionary perspective was Sri Aurobindo, who was particularly interested in the inner process of evolution as reflected in the evolution of human spirit or consciousness. See A. (Aryasamayajula) Ramamurty, *Vedanta and Its Philosophical Development*, pp. 123–125.
3 Transhumanists emphasize the possibility of human enhancement by science and technology. See *Humanity Plus Minus: Transhumanism and Its Critics*. However, while genetic engineering and other new techniques can possibly improve our intelligence, health and longevity, they cannot make us wiser or more virtuous. To transcend the present human condition and to develop morally and intellectually, we need a conscious cultural evolution.
4 See Steven Pinker, *The Better Angels of Our Nature*. Pinker describes a "pacification process" through which tribal warfare, feuding, and brigandry were brought under control by harsh laws, to be followed by a "civilizing process."
5 The Muslim Sufi poet and mystic Rumi envisaged human beings as emerging from lower forms of nature and evolving spiritually to higher angelic forms till their realization in God.
6 Julian Huxley, *Evolutionary Humanism*, pp. 105–106, 223–225.
7 Numbers following quotations refer to numbered paragraphs of the *Tractatus*.
8 See Harold Coward, *The Perfectibility of Human Nature*, p. 188.
9 Hans Morgenthau, *Politics Among Nations*, pp. 25–26.
10 Christopher Layne, "Kant or Cant: The Myth of Democratic Peace," s. 8–9.
11 Harold Coward, *The Perfectibility of Human Nature*, pp. 81–82.
12 See Thomas Hobbes, *Leviathan*.
13 See Nicholas Maxwell, *The Comprehensibility of the Universe*, p. 2.
14 Ibid., p. 217.
15 Ludwig Wittgenstein, *Tractatus Logico-Philosophicus*, 1.1; 1.2; 2.063.
16 See Julian Marias, *History of Philosophy*, pp. 342–343.
17 Fritjof Capra, *The Turning Point: Science, Society, and the Rising Culture*, p. 87.
18 Werner Heisenberg, *Physics and Philosophy*, p. 106.
19 Ibid., p. 199.
20 See Alexander Wendt, *Quantum Mind and Social Science*, p. 10.
21 Aristotle, *The Nicomachean Ethics*.
22 Fritjof Capra, *The Turning Point*, p. 268.
23 See Ann M. Kinney, *The Meaning of Dialectic in Plato*, p. 243.
24 See Roger Penrose, *The Road to Reality: A Complete Guide to the Laws of the Universe*, pp. 1014–1034.

1 Politics

1 Politics is the art of governing; it is essentially the organization of society for cooperation.

  1.1 The art of governing consists of both the ability to efficiently organize a society for joint action (cooperation) and the ability to keep oneself in power.

    1.11 The organization of society for cooperation is superior to keeping oneself in power, which is only a means to an end.

    1.12 Keeping oneself—be it a particular politician or a particular party—in power cannot become an end in itself.

    1.13 Keeping oneself in power is associated with a struggle for power, which occurs in political life to a greater or lesser extent, depending on the political system.

      1.131 Cooperation in a group requires leadership and presupposes a hierarchy, and the existence of these arouses jealousy and rivalry among some human beings resulting from their ambition, as well as from a desire for domination. In this way, an element of the struggle for power occurs in politics.

        1.1311 The desire for domination—the yearning to subjugate others and elevate oneself above them—is neither a primary impulse nor a natural feature of human beings. It destroys cooperation among them and leads them into conflict.

    1.14 The struggle for power plays a particular role in the multiparty political system of today's democracies and is a result of competition among persons, groups, or political parties.

1.15 The struggle for power—the conflict occurring both in the internal relations of a state and in international relations—is not the essence of politics, nor does it define politics; it is only one of its components.

    1.151 Social Darwinists and modern political realists identify conflict as a phenomenon that is essential to politics and even to life itself.

        1.1511 While conflict is certainly a part of the reality of life, it cannot be regarded as its essence.

        1.1512 If life were essentially conflict, then a world transformation would be impossible, there would be no progress, and nothing would ever grow.

        1.1513 Conflict is a part of life but is not its essence, and social progress and the improvement of human existence are possible.

        1.1514 Growth, development, and self-realization are the essence of human life.

1.16 Politics should not be reduced to the struggle for power or the art of winning the next election and maintaining oneself in power.

    1.161 Politics is not just "striving to share power or striving to influence the distribution of power, either among states or among groups within a state" and the state is not just "a relation of men dominating men" (Max Weber).

        1.1611 The struggle for power ultimately destroys politics proper and the desire for domination undermines political leadership and good government.

        1.6111 To define all politics as a struggle for power is not correct. Politics is not reducible to the struggle for power, which describes only one of its aspects.

    1.162 Although the essence of politics is not power or the struggle for power, no idea can be implemented in politics without adequate power.

1.163 As the art of governing, politics is a mixture of the ideas and forces that shape social life.

1.1631 Politics is not philosophy. While philosophy is about ideas, politics is about ideas and forces, for political ideas can be put into practice only if backed by sufficient force.

1.1632 Whoever mistakes politics for philosophy and tries to implement political ideas without calculating the relevant forces engages in wishful thinking, which usually ends in political disaster.

1.2 Politics is the ability to actualize a good life for a society.

1.21 Prosperity—a good life—is not only the wealth or material prosperity of human beings, but also their spiritual (moral and intellectual) development.

1.211 A good life comprehends the full human development.

1.22 For a pious person a good life is moral excellence and the knowing of God, and consequently the achievement of eternal happiness.

1.23 The highest goal of politics is the prosperity of the members of the political community—that is, of citizens.

1.231 The prosperity of citizens includes among other factors their wealth, security, health, and level of education, culture, and morality.

1.232 These factors—wealth, security, health, and level of education, culture, and morality in society—are interrelated.

1.2321 Security and wealth contribute to the increase of the level of education and culture of the members of the political community, but internal quarrels and moral decay lead to a deterioration of wealth and security.

1.3 There are two basic ways of organizing society: centralism and self-government.

1.31 In the case of centralism, decisions flow from the top to the bottom; in the case of self-government, decisions circulate from the top to the bottom and from the bottom to the top.

1.311 Centralism is associated with bureaucracy—the system of administration that limits individual initiative and is based on the application of rules and regulations laid down by the supreme authority.

1.312 Self-government is governing oneself—the system of administration based on independent decision-making by a particular community.

    1.3121 Self-government in a state requires the awakening of a civic spirit: that is, of the active involvement of citizens in the process of governance.

    1.3122 The awakening of the civic spirit is the essence of proper democracy, both direct and representative.

1.4 The art of governing pertains to the internal affairs of a particular state, as well as to the relations among states.

  1.41 Relations among states are defined by international politics.

    1.411 The main objective of international politics should be to build a strong international community.

    1.412 The goal for each state in the international arena is to work with other states and ensure its own safety and that of its citizens.

  1.42 The expression of effective international politics is the peaceful resolution of conflicts and improved relations among states in the international arena.

    1.421 War—the greatest catastrophe in human relations—should always be considered a last resort.

1.5 Cooperation (as opposed to conflict or the struggle for power) is the fundamental fact of human existence and the essence of politics.

  1.51 In their various activities, people strive for happiness or self-realization: that is, they try to satisfy their diverse needs. Such satisfaction depends on their ability to cooperate.

  1.52 Cooperation is based on the issues that unite people, as opposed to those that divide them.

1.521 Issues uniting people relate to the common good
or the public good.

1.522 So often, what one side proposes elicits an immediate protest from the other side. If politics is not
based on the common good, societies experience
divisiveness and quarreling.

1.53 Cooperation is based on companionship. Another name
for companionship is brotherhood.

1.531 Companionship is the principle of equality
between people who, because of differences in
their intelligence, education, social position, or
property, do not need to be equal.

1.54 Cooperation is based on the common good and common
values; it is destroyed by quarrels and hatred.

1.541 A society that is demoralized and internally
divided cannot function effectively and will not
be wealthy.

1.55 Cooperation is connected with a common goal, a common good, the division of labor, and specialization.

1.551 Even the conduct of war is based on cooperation,
rather than the reverse. The cooperation of citizens is needed in the event of war, and internal
conflict among them destroys their cooperation.

1.56 To provoke conflicts within societies and among nations
is an old method of ruling people, not for their common
good, but for the benefit of their enemies and of their
tyrants.

1.6 Politics transcends the boundaries of individual countries and
their mutual relations.

1.61 The supreme goal of supranational politics should be
to organize cooperation among people throughout the
entire world in order to advance peace and prosperity for
all humankind.

1.7 Any real politics is a result of human nature, as well as of a
specific culture and civilization.

1.71 Human action always relates to a specific cultural system
and a particular tradition.

1.711 To such a tradition belong those ideas from the
past that have entered into the consciousness of

successive generations and still continue to have an impact on their minds and actions.

1.712 In order to effectively change something and improve people's social and economic conditions, one needs to start from the existing tradition—that is, from what people believe—and then add new elements to it.

1.8 The world around us is constantly changing. Politics, as the art of governing, requires a thorough knowledge of human nature and human behavior, the continuous prediction of any accidents that may happen, and the ability to respond to them in a timely and appropriate manner.

1.9 In order to govern people, one needs to know them.

2   Human Nature

2 Human nature is unalterable.

  2.1 Human nature cannot be transformed by any revolutionary change.

    2.11 People, even though they are sometimes better, and then worse again, remain essentially the same.

  2.2 Human nature includes man and woman, and is the same regardless of gender.

  2.3 The continuity of human nature makes history repeat itself; therefore, we can discover some regularity in the history of humankind.

  2.4 The endurance of human nature does not, however, mean that there cannot be a qualitative change in human relationships, and that people cannot improve or, on the other hand, become more brutal.

    2.41 A positive qualitative change in human beings brings out their virtues, and virtues build a civilization; a negative change, conversely, brings civilization to ruin.

      2.411 Virtues are positive qualities of human character. Examples of virtues are industry, honesty, justice, sympathy, moderation, courage, and wisdom.

      2.412 The possession of virtues ennobles people: it improves them morally and intellectually, refines their desires, makes them independent from external influences, renders them spiritually stronger and resistant to the vicissitudes of life, and develops in them a positive attitude toward others.

      2.413 In opposition to virtues are vices, such as greed, selfishness, jealousy, deceit, lust, sloth, vulgarity, cruelty, and ignorance—the characteristics of mediocre and wicked people.

2.42 Depending on whether or not they improve and acquire virtues, people can be the source of the greatest good or the greatest evil to each other.

2.43 An excellent, fully civilized society is a society of virtue. It consists of ennobled people, cooperating with each other and sharing a sense of community.

2.5 Human nature is a set of dispositions or abilities. It is not a specific feature of human character, such as a virtue or a vice.

2.51 People are endowed with reason. They have a natural ability to think. They are "persons," that is, beings of a rational nature, who guide themselves on their own.

2.511 Personality implies dignity. As rational beings, who realize their own selves and who are not merely a means to something else, human beings have a special dignity.

2.512 Reason, the ability to conceptually grasp reality and formulate and verify theories, is a special feature of human beings, which distinguishes them from other living beings.

2.513 Human reason cannot be reduced to its purely instrumental function, i.e., thinking about the optimal use of available resources to achieve specific goals; instead, it also includes a reflection on what is true and what is false, what is beneficial and what is harmful, what is beautiful and what is ugly, and what is good and what is bad.

2.514 Only human beings are able to seek the truth, to see beauty and harmony in the world, to engage in moral reflection, and to reflect on their own lives.

2.52 In view of their ability to deliberate on ethical issues, people are not only rational beings, but also moral beings.

2.521 Only in the human world does there exist a difference between good and evil, that is, the sphere of morality. Also, only in reference to the human being can we talk about moral degradation.

2.522 People can improve morally and intellectually. Thanks to the influence of their social environment, to their education, and to their own efforts, all human beings can become morally better.

2.523 "Right reason" is a human capacity for rational thought about what is beneficial and what is not, what is morally good and what is evil, and for choosing what is beneficial and good.

2.524 Discussing moral issues and considering what is right in a particular case, we are closer to each other as people and very different from other animals.

2.525 There is nothing more opposed to human nature than vicious deeds. Because of vices, people may distort their character, but through honesty, sympathy, charity, justice, wisdom, and other virtues, they can achieve moral perfection.

2.526 The human being who departs from morality and reason is one who becomes wicked, fallen, or brutal. Wickedness, fallenness, and brutality are three successive stages of demoralization.

2.5261 Wicked people are individuals who harm others and use lies, deception, and bribery to achieve their malicious, socially harmful goals.

2.5262 Fallen people are those in whom there is an inability to rise above their animality and resist their own temptations and desires.

2.5263 Brutal people are those who have shed all moral consideration toward other people. Brutality manifests itself in cruelty that may be directed at even a stranger, a passerby, or an innocent child. It is a denial of human nature.

2.53 Human beings are by nature social beings. They have a natural disposition to live in a society, cooperate with others, and reap the benefits of social life.

2.531 The individual as a stand-alone being is a fiction.

2.5311 No single human being can ever achieve anything by his own efforts alone, unsupported by other people.

2.5312 Human beings are not self-sufficient. Basic human needs—food, shelter, security, offspring—can be satisfied only by means of cooperation, and only through cooperation can human beings build their culture.

2.5313 Humans beings can achieve success only through cooperation with others; alone, the human being is at best only free.

2.532 Human beings never act alone. However, even a single person can be a powerful force for modifying the operation of society.

2.5321 The individual is the source of all creativity and all inventions.

2.5322 With the support of others, a single individual of great intellect is able to change the entire world.

2.5323 Great individuals and great masses make history equally.

2.533 Living in a society and cooperating to achieve common goals are for people something natural, as is their ability to think rationally and achieve moral improvement.

2.5331 People do not join the community on the basis of an agreement, as claimed by Hobbes, Locke, and other theorists of the social contract. Human beings have always lived in communities.

2.534 Reasoning, sharing thoughts and feelings, learning from and teaching others, and exchanging and discussing ideas connect human beings in their natural brotherhood.

2.535 Ties of brotherhood connecting people are a result of the unity of their nature and their common goal.

2.5351 All people have the same basic needs and are endowed with the same mental powers, though in unequal degrees. All have the same goal, which is happiness or self-realization, although it may be expressed in different ways.

2.5352 Self-realization is expressed most fully in moral and intellectual perfection.

2.54 It belongs to the nature of the human being to be able to create culture.

2.541 Culture is an artificial, human-made environment—material, social, and spiritual—by which human beings achieve their objectives. It is both a set of means to fulfill the simplest human needs and a constantly evolving system of new aims, new values, and new creative possibilities.

2.5411 People do not live in an abstract environment, but in the environment of a particular culture, which consists of the economic system, education, morality, law, politics, entertainment, philosophy, religion, science, and art.

2.542 Culture consists of organized activities by which human beings transcend the limitations associated with their original, natural animal endowment.

2.5421 Culture can be used for both constructive and destructive goals. Slavery and war are the results of the development of culture, just as are science and art.

2.543 Rules of behavior developed within the context of culture—orders and prohibitions—are an important instrument of human freedom. However, they may also become a tool of oppression and discrimination.

2.5431 Discrimination is the exclusion of some people from action because of their race, ethnicity, gender, or religion.

2.5432 Oppression is the limitation of someone's freedom by the imposition of excessive burdens or obligations.

2.5433 There is a difference between the laws of liberty—rules developed in the course of tradition that serve the development of the individual and of society—and the laws of tyranny—rules artificially imposed from above that limit freedom and impede such development.

2.55 Because of the culture that they form, human beings are by nature free.

2.551 Animal life consists in obedience to biological drives. Culture creates a new environment in which freedom is generated—freedom, which consists of the increasing control of human beings over themselves and their environment.

2.552 People can grow beyond their animality, control their desires, and create moral principles governing their conduct.

2.5521 Human beings are not driven to action only by hunger, thirst, or the need to sleep. Ethical, religious, and intellectual values produced by culture are new driving forces for human action.

2.5522 Because of their culture, human beings take action not only because of biological desires, which they are able to a significant degree to control, but also because of the values that they accept. They are driven to action not only by basic desires, but also by learned behaviors and specific rules of action.

2.553 The development of culture knows no boundaries.

2.5531 Culture requires a constant rebirth—a modification, as new aspects of life arise—and an ascent from generation to generation; if it continues unchanged, it becomes obsolete.

2.5532 Everything living is changing; and if a living being becomes immobile, it suffocates and finally dies.

2.5533 The liveliness of culture depends on its continual revival.

2.554 Modern philosophy conveys to us a mechanical picture of the human being driven by desires. Such a picture is found not only in Hobbes and his successors, but also in the utilitarians and behaviorists. It has in addition penetrated the thinking of Hans Morgenthau and other theorists of political realism, for whom human beings are self-interested individuals, desirous of power. Out of this picture emerges an inadequate image of politics as a struggle for power.

2.5541 The human being is not a simple mechanism whose operation can be reduced to the pursuit of pleasure and the avoidance of suffering, or to selfishness and the struggle for power, but rather a complex organism of an axiological character. With the culture and values he creates, he has the ability to transform his desires and to control them.

2.555 Values are traits or qualities that human beings appreciate because of their usefulness or their role in the satisfaction of human needs (vital, material, intellectual, aesthetic, religious, etc.), regardless of whether they refer to a specific person, thing, property, procedure, social position, field of knowledge, or character trait.

2.5551 Values are described by words such as "useful," "pleasant," "noble," "beautiful," and their opposites by words such as "useless," "unpleasant," "ignoble," "awful."

2.5552 Culture creates values, and in a particular culture there occurs a continuous dispute about values—about the recognition of some as important and the rejection of others.

2.55521 In the culture developed by the Classical Tradition, at the top of the hierarchy of values there is virtue and the knowledge of God.

2.556 Interests are the pursuits of things considered valuable.

2.5561 In the course of the development of culture, human interests undergo sublimation: from the material, related to the satisfaction of biological and physical needs, to the spiritual, related to the mental development of the individual.

2.6 Education has a great impact on the development of human beings.

  2.61 Human beings are largely what education makes of them.

  2.62 The aim of the education of the human being is the development of his physical and mental fitness and his ability to live in harmony with others and cooperate with them in a society.

  2.63 A fully educated individual is a person who is erudite in knowledge and noble in character; equipped with traditional knowledge, while capable of using the tools of modern technology; able to take the initiative and express his own opinion; steadfast in difficult moments and capable of standing up for the values on which civilization is based.

  2.64 The behavior of individuals is affected by their personal qualities, as well as their cultural environment and civilization.

2.7 People are always part of a particular culture and civilization.

  2.71 Universal man, a favorite subject of many philosophers and political scientists, is a pure abstraction that in reality does not exist.

  2.72 Like culture, civilization is a system and environment of social life. It is the way of life of a particular people and the material, social, and spiritual environment created by them.

  2.73 Civilization represents (1) a culture that reaches a higher level of material, social, and spiritual development; (2) a specific civilization, such as the Chinese, Indian, Arab, or traditional Western European.

  2.74 Civilizations include extensive, supranational collections of people and may incorporate societies representing various language groups and cultures.

  2.75 The development of civilizations does not progress along a single path. It is accomplished by the development of independent cultures that come into contact and mutually influence one another.

2.76 The primary carrier of an independent culture that is common to a community is the nation.

    2.761 The nation is a community that, over the course of history, has developed a common culture and is linked by a sense of a common identity.

2.77 The character of a civilization expresses itself in the worldview with which it is imbued and which it implements.

    2.771 There is no one perfect model of the civilizational development of humanity, nor any one society that can be a perfect model for all others. A universal civilization encompassing all humankind does not exist.

    2.772 Countries heterogeneous in terms of civilization, or those that lack a developed, coherent national or religious culture, decline.

2.8 Today's Western European civilization is a mixture of civilizations. The West is not a single civilization, but remains under the mutually eradicating influences of the classical-Christian civilization, the oriental-Byzantine civilization, and the militaristic civilization. We will call these, for short, Classicism, Byzantism, and Militarism.

2.81 At the core of the classical-Christian civilization (Classicism), which is the traditional Western European civilization, is the Classical Tradition.

    2.811 The Classical Tradition is a moral tradition that emerged in Western political thought. It was developed by Plato and Aristotle, and includes thinkers for whom politics is intrinsically linked with ethics, and who emphasize the importance of virtue for public life.

    2.812 The Classical Tradition was continued by Christian thinkers. Many influential philosophers, and in particular St. Thomas Aquinas, sought to reconcile the classical and Christian political and ethical concepts.

    2.813 The Classical Tradition is conceptually closely related to some non-European schools of political thought. The role of virtue in politics was emphasized by Manu in India, by Confucius in China, and by Al-Farabi in the Muslim world, as well as by other great political thinkers of the East.

2.8131 The Classical Tradition has transcended its classical-Christian origins and is the common heritage of all humanity.

2.82 Classicism is based on personalism, individual initiative, self-government, autonomy, and diversity. It creates a society of an organic character. Its expression is the philosophy of solidarity, which recognizes each person's dignity and requires that each person should be treated as an end in himself, and not a means to an end.

2.83 The characteristic features of Byzantism are the ubiquity of the state, centralism, uniformity, standardization, and bureaucracy. Byzantism is based on the belief that everything can be achieved by means of laws, regulations, orders, and prohibitions. It dampens individual initiative and creates a society of mechanical character, subjected to the state.

2.84 At the basis of Militarism is enmity. Enmity can be fabricated using such tools as fear mongering and propaganda, and can turn peaceful people into the hate-filled cogs of a war machine. Militarism creates a society ready for conquest. The individual has value only as a member of an organization.

2.841 A typical example of a militarized society was that of Prussia. In the Prussian tradition, in which the idea of individual freedom never appears, and with which the Nazis identified themselves, the fear of authority is used as an instrument to transform people into the obedient elements of a war machine—troops who obey orders without hesitation and without questioning.

2.8411 In a militarized society, where the main virtues are obedience, discipline, and subordination to authority, the most important value is the state and its military power; any human individuality that does not serve the state is of no value.

2.842 Enmity is not an innate feature of human beings, but it can be instilled through culture. Its development in a society is the result of dominant ideas we find within that society and the application of indoctrination techniques. It is an expression of the philosophy of the enemy, which is the negation of the philosophy of solidarity.

2.843 At present, many conflicts are being played out in the world. The specialists in playing out these conflicts, from which they derive benefits for themselves, are the players.

2.8431 The basic strategy for each country today should be to get out of the game.

2.85 Between Classicism, Byzantism, and Militarism there occurs an eternal struggle. Their accommodation in one society on the basis of the principles of multiculturalism and egalitarianism is not possible. The character of public life in a given country and, in the long run, the future character of humanity depend on which of the three civilizations prevails.

2.9 The goal of all states should be to work together for the sake of the security, peace, and prosperity of all humankind.

3   The State

3 The state is a territorial political organization based on a society.

   3.1 The existence of the state is associated with a particular territory, inhabited by a certain people, and a set of political institutions (the government, the military, the police, and the courts) that are responsible for organizing and upholding the social order in that territory.

      3.11 The essence of an organization lies in the authority that exists within it. This authority signifies not only a certain social status, but also power, enabling decision-making.

      3.12 The institution of the state presupposes the existence of political power and an apparatus of coercion, but the state cannot be identified with them.

         3.121 Max Weber's definition of the state as "a compulsory association which organizes domination" (*anstaltsmäßiger Herrschaftsverband*)—the organization of society based on coercion—is not adequate.

         3.122 Coercion is a means of control that is essential for the effective cooperation of a group. It emerges in the educational process of developing the ability to cooperate, as well as in cooperation itself.

         3.123 "There is much more to a state than a claimed monopoly on the legitimate use of physical force or coercion in a territory" (Christopher Morris).

      3.13 The purpose of the state is not coercion, but the cooperation, liberty, prosperity, and security of its citizens.

         3.131 In an ideal world—and such is defined by the existence of a virtuous citizenry—we still need governments, but in this situation states that employ little or no coercion are conceivable.

3.2 The state is based on a society and serves it.

  3.21 A society, community, or group is a set of individuals linked together. They can be connected by a common identity, locality, ethnicity, or nationality, or by ties of friendship or common interest.

    3.211 A society is a diverse community. It consists of people who differ from each other in their level of affluence, intelligence, and education, as well as their character traits.

    3.212 Being as it is a diverse community, a society does not have the capacity to fully develop without a variety of social layers or classes.

      3.2121 Classes (social layers) are groups of people differing in wealth, education, employment, values, and traditions.

      3.2122 The separation of people into classes in a society is a natural process and has its basis in differences between people, in their possession in varying degrees of such attributes as courage, ambition, intelligence, and resourcefulness.

      3.2123 Classes are not rigid castes into which a person is born and continues to be imprisoned throughout life. In an open society, the social composition of classes is constantly changing.

      3.2124 Despite the impact of egalitarian ideologies, a classless society has never been fully realized and never will be realized in practice. Because of human ambition and the need to distinguish oneself from others, new classes will always arise in the place of old ones.

      3.2125 A classless society can only be an artifice.

      3.2126 A diversity of people, social classes, cultures, religions, and nations, melded together through cooperation, comprises a variety of complementary skills, talents, experiences, and values.

3.213 The exclusion of a certain class from society, in the form of its abolition, marginalization, or removal from influence in political and economic life, results in a rejection of the values that it represents.

3.2131 Any exclusion enforced from above, and thus artificially, is a denial of freedom and introduces into a society an element of tyranny.

3.2132 A classless society is a tyranny. Even a democracy may become a tyranny, if processes within it lead to the removal from political and economic life of certain classes or groups that can enhance cooperation in a society.

3.214 The basic values of the three main classes of contemporary society—labor, business, and honor—are freedom, entrepreneurship, and nobility. All these values should be present in a well-organized society and should be represented by certain social groups.

3.2141 The civilizational development of a society is based on the contribution of all its parts, that is, of all classes or social layers. It is not correct when certain classes are excluded from social life, or when one class politically or economically dominates the others.

3.2142 Entrepreneurship should always be protected against bureaucracy.

3.21421 The bureaucrat represents an order; the entrepreneur, initiative. The bureaucrat gets a salary; the entrepreneur generates an income.

3.21422 The bureaucrat will never understand the entrepreneur, and vice versa. Therefore, they must tolerate and respect each other.

3.215 The inevitability of class struggle is a dogma. Social classes can work together.

3.216 As long as social classes are incorporated into the structure of an open society, the division of society into different classes will tend to promote its development.

   3.2161 An open society is one in which all people are given the chance to advance from a lower to a higher social position.

   3.2162 Every person should have the opportunity to compete for a better place in society, and the prospect of promotion from one class to another.

   3.2163 The basis for social advancement should always lie in an individual's own attributes and efforts: his intelligence, activity, entrepreneurship, resourcefulness, virtue, and merit.

3.22 The government of a state is always run with a view to a specific purpose and is limited by this purpose.

   3.221 The purpose of a government is not limited to the protection of the life, liberty, and property of individuals, as stated by Locke. Its primary task stems from the first principle of humanity, which is cooperation.

      3.2211 People unite into communities not only for "comfortable, safe, and peaceable living one amongst another, in a secure enjoyment of their properties" (John Locke), but in fact primarily to work together for the common benefit.

   3.222 The main purposes of the state are the cooperation, liberty, prosperity, and security of citizens.

   3.223 The basic functions of the government are, first, to maintain a balance between the various classes, groups, institutions, and interests within society; second, to enforce compliance of the law and internal order; and third, to provide defense against external aggression.

3.224 The most important good that the state provides is security—that is, internal and external peace—because the development of culture and the flourishing of all other goods depend on it.

3.23 The greatest detriment to society and the biggest crisis it can experience is war.

3.231 War abolishes laws that customarily regulate human relationships and replaces constructive human behavior, based on cooperation, with criminality.

3.232 In view of their consequences for society, wars should always be avoided as far as is possible; only defensive or limited wars, engaging society to a small degree, should be fought.

3.2321 A war between states cannot be avoided by concessions, and even less so by the propaganda of hatred and the escalation of hostility.

3.2322 Peace is a dynamic state of resolving existing differences of interest among people.

3.3 The state is a politically organized society; it is a political community—a community of people organized under a particular regime.

3.31 A political regime is the type of political organization of a society.

3.311 A political regime is more than a form of government. It defines not only a political institutional arrangement—the governmental institutions that exist in a state—but also a political culture that is created by those institutions—the values that exist in a given society.

3.312 The political regimes (or forms of government) most frequently mentioned by political philosophers are monarchy, aristocracy, democracy, oligarchy, tyranny, and polity—a mixed regime.

3.313 Political regimes are either correct or defective. In correct regimes, those who hold power rule their countries for the sake of the common good; in defective ones, they rule for their own benefit or for that of a particular class or political party.

3.4 When carrying out its functions properly, the state creates a social environment in which culture develops and people—its citizens—can live a good life.

   3.41 The ultimate goal of state policy is a good life or prosperity—that is, to make possible the comprehensive development of its citizens: material, moral, and intellectual.

   3.411 A good life is a complete life.

      3.4111 All people have the right to develop their natural talents and utilize their acquired skills, so long as these contribute to their personal development and do not cause harm to others.

  3.42 Depending on what people are learning and what they are accustomed to in a given state, it can be considered either good or defective.

   3.421 The good state is a just state.

   3.422 In a good state, individuals can develop their unique personalities, and the educational system and laws promote cooperation and virtuous practices; in a defective one, private interest dominates the common good, and education and legislation demoralize citizens.

   3.423 The good state is one that fulfills its functions and enables its citizens to satisfy their needs. Citizens can identify with such a state and say with pride, "This is my country."

   3.424 In a good or just state, all individuals, groups, and social classes strive for happiness, as they best understand it, but never at the expense of others.

   3.425 The good state supports the physical and spiritual development of human beings. It creates an environment for human self-realization, where people can cooperate with one another and in which they develop a particular culture.

   3.426 The good state is the protector of society, not its master, or, even worse, its destroyer.

   3.427 Left to themselves, without any moral signposts, individuals often choose targets unworthy of human beings. The good state directs citizens to the path of virtuous action and cooperation; the defective state, instead of improving them, corrupts them.

3.43 In order to be good, the state must be strong. The power of a state is the result of the strength of its economy, defensive capabilities, and civic virtues.

3.431 A society that is internally divided by quarrels leads to a weak state. The costs of living in a weak state are paid by all its citizens.

3.432 The weak state does not protect citizens from internal and external dangers. Such a state is threatened with collapse.

3.433 A collapse of the state that occurs as a result of political naivety and mistakes is even harder to accept than the death of a close friend. It is a great tragedy. When a state collapses, it is as if a world were ending.

3.434 The weak state cannot be free; and if it seems to be free, this is only an illusion.

3.44 The good state is not indifferent to the fates of other states and their citizens. It participates in the activities of international society and in providing humanitarian assistance to world society. Thus, it fulfills the ideal of global solidarity.

3.441 Members of international society are states that are united by certain common values and a willingness to cooperate and form international organizations; members of world society are all human beings living on the Earth.

3.45 The good state does not conduct wars, unless to defend weaker states or itself.

3.46 The activities of states and other actors on the international scene are subject to moral judgment.

3.47 States, like people, pursue specific interests.

3.471 As in the case of individuals, we cannot expect states to abstain from actions that bring them benefit. They are not required to sacrifice their own interests for those of others, or to surrender to others what they need for themselves. They can engage in competition against others and devote all their efforts to winning. But what brings them benefit should not be associated with injustice and harm to others.

3.48 Almost any state is better than no state at all. The maintenance of peaceful and prosperous life requires a government capable of implementing order and providing security.

3.5 The condition of the state depends not only on material factors but also, and primarily, on the moral strength of society.

3.51 States and civilizations typically experience growth, followed by a period of decline.

3.511 The penalty for the moral decay of society—for the disappearance of civic virtues—is the collapse of states and civilizations.

3.512 States do not usually die because of invasions from the outside, but rather because of weakness and corruption attacking them from the inside.

3.513 Any society can, even within a single generation, be morally corrupted from top to bottom by means of indoctrination and bad government.

3.52 The repair of states and civilizations can be undertaken through the moral improvement of individuals and societies.

3.53 In order to predict the future of a given state, it is not enough to assess its current economic and military strength. We need to ask: what are its citizens' ideas, what are their morals, and what trends prevail in their education?

3.531 Prophesying the future based on economic data and geopolitical considerations alone, without reference to civic virtues, is pure fantasy; likewise, projects to repair societies that consist exclusively in institutional changes and do not take into account moral and educational factors are dangerous utopias.

3.54 The greatness of a state depends not on the size of its territory and the extent of its military power, but on the qualities that it represents. The more its policies enable citizens' well-being and contribute to the common good of all humanity, the more it deserves to be called great.

3.6 The state is the political organization of a society, and the nation, its cultural unity.

   3.61 Cultural unity consists in the common language, traditions, and customs of a given society. It is expressed in the everyday human contacts related to family life, social relationships, work, and entertainment, as well as in certain commonly accepted values, such as freedom, justice, and honor.

   3.62 The differentiation of humanity into nations is the basis of its progress. Each nation develops its own culture—its way of life. This diversity of cultures influencing each other is a creative element.

      3.621 The nation is the broadest social group united by the same type of culture, and one that develops as a whole.

         3.6211 Common to the members of one nation are their language, history, traditions, customary law, and religious and social values.

         3.6212 Nations are not created artificially. The nation and the family are natural communities that cannot be replaced by any artificial construction without loss to the development of civilization.

         3.6213 The nation can be replaced neither by a political organization, which is the state, nor by an artificially created democratic society.

         3.6214 The dissolution of national culture caused by an external factor—for example, by laws that prevent people from observing their ancient customs—is the abolition of freedom.

         3.6215 The importance of a nation to the rest of humanity is the result of the creative force of its culture. It depends on what the nation possesses, what it has achieved so far, what it is capable of, and what its contribution to the civilizational development of other nations has been.

3.63 Many historians consider nationality as a phenomenon associated with the history of modern Europe. However, being a nation (or a tribe, or another group united by a common culture) is an original and fundamental phenomenon in the history of humankind.

3.64 The nation can exist as a nation-state, but the state and the nation are not the same.

    3.641 In the case where the state borders extend along the boundaries of one culture, so that the state and nation overlap each other, we are dealing with a nation-state.

        3.6411 The nation-state is a unit of cultural cooperation.

        3.6412 A nation-state, associated with one civilization and one culture, forms a strong political organization.

    3.642 "In the unity of civilization there lies the success of strong nations. This is the basis of real power that can withstand the pressure of time" (Feliks Koneczny).

        3.6421 The most powerful political organizations are based on the interrelation of social groups that cooperate with each other because of their common language, traditions, customs, and values.

    3.643 In one state there may be several nations that, although they have different cultures, are based on one civilization; and yet, there cannot be several mutually exclusive civilizations within a state without internal tensions and threats to the integrity of that state.

    3.644 Civilizations that are hostile to each other can, in terms of their actions, at best remain mutually indifferent to each other. Their conflict within a state leads to an inner division of society, and consequently to the weakening and eventual collapse of the state.

    3.645 In a case where different civilizations coexist within one state, there are only two possible forms of peaceful cooperation for them: the domination of one, more tolerant civilization over the rest; or the equal subjection of all to a dictatorship that aims at social peace.

3.6451 Historical experience shows that in cases where there exists a diversity of civilizations, it is usually impossible to maintain the unity of the state. As an example, we can give the former Yugoslavia, where, despite the similarity of the language and many common traditions, the diversity of civilization, as a higher power, forced Croats and Serbs into a fratricidal fight not long after the death of the dictator Tito. This sudden development surprised even the combatants themselves. A similar scenario is a threat to all artificial multicivilizational assemblages.

3.6452 A dictatorship that is tolerant of cultural diversity, or an authoritarian government whose purpose is to ensure social peace, is a better regime than a weak democracy riven by civilizational conflict that ends in civil war.

3.6453 For the sake of its unity and effectiveness, the state should always be based on a native national culture and one civilization, while maintaining tolerance toward all others.

3.65 The concept of the nation is not highly regarded today by many people because it is often equated with nationalism, ethnic cleansing, and war. However, this view is wrong. Nationalism in its extreme form of chauvinism, which fills people with hatred toward others and makes them belligerent, is in fact an enemy of the nation. It is an obstacle to the development of culture and prevents individuals and groups from realizing their desired way of life.

3.651 The nation is a bearer of culture and a tool of freedom. In the nation itself there is nothing aggressive or destructive. The nation is best protected from internal conflict and external aggression when it is organized as a nation-state.

3.6511 The real downside of nationalism comes into play only when a heated conflict of cultural or civilizational character occurs within a country, or when one nation refuses the right to self-determination to another.

3.6512 An external danger related to nationalism occurs when the cultural forces of one nation are converted for aggressive military purposes.

3.652 A state that is based on cultural unity can emotionally engage large masses of people to unite around common goals, and will therefore have adequate strength, which can be used for war and conquest.

3.6521 Conquest is the subjugation of one nation (one culture) by another one through force or cunning, resulting in the incorporation of one country, its territory, or at least its political or economic system, into another.

3.6522 Conquest combines the benefits of plunder and slavery. The winners provide political and economic leadership, and the conquered, natural resources and manpower.

3.653 Educated toward hatred and turned in the direction of conquest, a society that under normal, peaceful conditions would develop its own culture loses its freedom and is transformed into an instrument for attaining military goals.

3.6531 As a result of indoctrination, stimulating enmity and militancy, nationalism—an emotional attachment to one's own nation and a desire for its cultural autonomy—turns into chauvinism, hostility toward other nations, or imperialism, subjugation of other nations.

3.6532 Extreme nationalism, chauvinism, and imperialism, which are expressions of Militarism, constitute a denial of the fundamental principle of nationhood, which is its self-determination—that is, its free development.

3.6533 Militarism leads to the ruin of the nation in which it prevails and, on the international scale, to the destruction of humanity.

3.654 A nation-state, the defender of its own freedom and culture, is a dynamic cultural and civilizational entity. In order to maintain its own social development, it needs peace. When it does go forth to fight, it fights for its own freedom and for the freedom of others. It is opposed to the chauvinistic and imperialist state that mobilizes its people to aggression.

3.7 When a state maintains a continuous readiness for war, this state of mind pervades every aspect of human life, and nation, freedom, and democracy all die.

3.71 As Thucydides warned us many centuries ago, war is a brutal teacher of evil. The evil of war is not only the destruction of life and other catastrophic consequences in the form of disease, poverty, and social disorganization. War also leads to the collapse of culture and the decay of moral principles.

3.72 In time of war, only those who are participating in a just defensive war and who follow the rules of honor and other ethical rules of warfare can preserve their moral integrity.

3.8 When it is properly organized, the state serves the whole society. Only in defective political regimes does the state become an apparatus of coercion serving a particular individual, group, party, or class, or an omnipotent bureaucracy.

3.81 In faulty and internally torn states there develops class egoism, growing out of the rule of one class. In contrast, a good or just state is based on the cooperation of classes. In such a state, citizens, groups, parties, and classes work together for the common good.

3.82 The good state, which allows citizens to improve themselves morally and to know God, is, according to Al-Farabi, the virtuous or excellent state, one that actualizes the highest goal of human life. This state can be contrasted with the unconscious state, whose citizens are not aware of their highest purpose—eternal happiness—and equate happiness merely with health, wealth, bodily pleasures, honors, or social status; beyond that, it can be contrasted with states that are capricious and confused, whose inhabitants once knew about their highest goal, but then fell under the influence of new ideas and forgot or falsely transformed it; and lastly, it can be contrasted with the vicious state, in which there is a conscious rejection of God and of moral principles grounded in religion and tradition.

3.821 Al-Farabi categorized democratic countries as being among the unconscious or ignorant states; however, Western democracies today are in fact confused states. Forgetting about the Christian roots of their culture and civilization, many of their inhabitants have adopted secular religions in the form of the gospel of Marx, the worship of money, a mirage of multiculturalism, or an illusion of the religiously neutral state.

3.822 The importance of religion lies in the fact that it shapes the character of human beings, influences their moral education, builds their community of values, produces solidarity among them, and fills their minds with a higher content than do the things of everyday life.

3.823 The inner emptiness of people in the West today, the effect of their consumerization and secularization, is waiting to be refilled, and their spirit to be uplifted.

3.9 As the bearer of culture and civilization, the good state, serving society and making possible the self-realization of its citizens, is an actualization of freedom.

4 Freedom

4 Freedom is the possibility of self-realization of the individual and the society, based on choice.

   4.1 Freedom means self-determination—having power over oneself—and is associated with making decisions, having the possibility of choice, and directing one's own actions.

      4.11 In contrast to coercion and servitude, where one is subject to the decisions of others, freedom is the ability to decide for oneself.

         4.111 Free people are those who are capable of making decisions related to what they believe, what they say, and what they do.

      4.12 Contrary to popular opinion, freedom is not:

        a. doing what we like;
        b. absence of restraint.

         4.121 Freedom is not license—doing what one likes.

            4.1211 The freedom of individuals does not give them the right to do anything they wish—they have no right to insult and destroy each other, to harm others, or to enslave or conquer them.

         4.122 Freedom is not related to the absence of restraint, but to a conscious choice. The essence of freedom is to accept those constraints on human action that allow human beings to achieve their own desired goals, not those artificially imposed on them.

4.1221 Freedom does not consist in disrespecting traditional practices or customs, insofar as they are conducive to social life and contribute to the common benefit, but rather in accepting them, acting in accordance with them, and assigning values to them.

4.1222 Human beings who in their actions are directed by their conscience are free. Conscience, an internal constraint on action, is not a limitation of freedom.

4.123 Hobbes defines freedom as the absence of restraint; that is, of external impediments (in the form of the law) and internal constraints (in the form of conscience). He is rightly criticized by Locke, who writes that "freedom is not, as we are told, a liberty for every man to do what he lists . . . but liberty to dispose, and order as he lists, his person, actions, possessions, and his whole property, within the allowance of those laws under which he is."

4.1231 However, laws enacted by the state do not always make people free.

4.2 There are laws of liberty, and there are laws of tyranny.

4.21 The laws of liberty are rules for successful action—action that brings benefits to the individual or group and is not associated with doing harm to other human beings.

4.22 The laws of tyranny are rules that are artificially imposed on people and challenge their traditions and experience. For their practical implementation, such rules typically require indoctrination and coercion.

4.23 Culture, a part of which is the laws that are mandatory in a given state, imposes restraints on people. Compliance with certain restraints that are dictated by culture, such as rules or standards related to education or the conduct of economic activities, is necessary for achieving successful action, just as it is necessary to obey the laws of physics or biology.

4.231 The orders and prohibitions growing out of a tradition can serve freedom. They arise from an experience of cooperation. They can impose a strict discipline on human endeavors without being laws of tyranny.

4.24 The difference between freedom and enslavement lies in the fact that in the case of the former, the restraints of a given culture are necessary for successful action and the development of the human personality and human skills, but in the case of the latter, they prevent joint action, limit the development of human beings, and serve the few at the expense of the many.

4.241 Enslavement occurs in situations in which effort is required of others, while initiative and benefit sharing are taken away from them, and in which individuals are made into a means to an end.

4.242 People who are freed from the influence of religion and tradition have seemingly limitless possibilities of achieving their goals, of growing wealthy, and of satisfying individual desires. However, their freedom is often illusory. Their mutual selfishness prevents them from cooperating effectively.

4.2421 In the process of transforming the world, the West has transformed itself. It has freed itself from the traditional constraints that kept human appetites in check, and has allowed individuals the unlimited pursuit of their own individual desires.

4.2422 Individuals who are not restricted by religion and tradition lose their current culture and revert to a state of primitive animality—a way of life dominated by impulses and desires.

4.2423 Deprived of religion and tradition, life lacks a higher goal.

4.25 In order for the laws enacted by the state to be laws of liberty, they must be based on natural law.

4.251 The laws of nature describe and explain the behavior of natural forces. They are also incorporated into culture in the form of natural law.

4.252 Natural law defines the rules of conduct of the individual in coexistence with other people. Its provisions are universally applicable moral norms that are neither revealed nor constituted, but are the result of right reason, available to human beings through the innate strength of their own minds.

4.253 In order to skillfully organize their lives and pass this form of organization on to future generations, human beings must learn to distinguish what is beneficial from what is deleterious, what is useful from what is harmful, and what is just from what is unjust.

4.254 Natural law, whose basic principle is doing no harm to others, is connected with a moral sense of what is right and what is wrong.

4.255 As expressed concisely by St. Thomas Aquinas, the natural law commands: "Good is to be done and ensued, and evil is to be avoided."

4.3 The more members of a society have the chance for self-realization, the more complete is their freedom in that society.

4.31 Freedom is the possibility of self-realization; happiness or self-realization is the realization of human needs.

4.311 Freedom consists in the possibility of satisfying the primary biological needs of individuals as well as their derivative needs in the context of an organized society.

4.3111 With the development of culture, simple biological needs related to human physiology are supplemented by new needs related to possession of the proper tools, equipment, clothing, housing, education, knowledge, occupation, or estate, or the appropriate social position.

4.312 People also have the need to live in a safe, peaceful environment conducive to the preservation of their life, liberty, and property, to the improvement of their character, and to the expansion of their knowledge, so that they can know themselves, the world, and God.

4.32 The self-realization of the individual, namely the satisfaction of needs in private life, defines the limits of government action; and then, the self-realization of society, which is the self-realization of other individuals and the fulfillment of the requirements of the public good, defines the limits of individual freedom.

4.33 Freedom, as the possibility of self-realization, gives people satisfaction with their achievements and, along with this, a sense of their personal worth.

> 4.331 If the possibility of self-realization is given to the few and taken from others, then this is not what we would call freedom, but its denial—enslavement.
>
> > 4.3311 Freedom is associated with equal access to education, employment, property, and public life, and the equitable sharing of benefits; enslavement is associated with exploitation, injustice, and the monopolization of politics, wealth, information, and the media.
>
> 4.332 Although distribution of the benefits of joint action does not need to be equal, it must be just or equitable; that is, it must be proportional to the initiative employed, the effort, and the work. The basis for the equitable sharing of benefits is the satisfaction of all individuals or other parties involved in a joint action.

4.34 Unemployment is one of the most harmful forms of the denial of freedom related to the use of personal skills and abilities. Regardless of whether unemployed people receive an allowance or not, they are not fully free because they cannot perform the work for which they have been educated, nor can they receive the reward for it—a reward that would give them self-esteem.

4.4 Freedom is a gift of culture, and culture is the gift of freedom.

> 4.41 Freedom is essential for maintaining tradition and mobilizing human talent. The progress of culture and civilization is not possible without freedom, without the possibility of human self-realization.
>
> 4.42 Freedom is the condition that enables us to enjoy the achievements of culture and to sustain its development.

4.5 Freedom presupposes that initiative, criticism, and even dissent remain unfettered.

4.51 Indoctrination is an attempt at bringing about a complete submission of minds to a certain doctrine or a particular set of views. To implement its purpose, it uses the education system and the media. It stifles initiative and criticism.

4.511 Effective indoctrination requires a monopoly on the dissemination of information. The antidote to this monopoly is freedom of speech, which is essential for the formation of individual and collective intentions.

4.52 Free political discussion is an indispensable condition for the development of culture. More harm is done to society by restrictions on freedom of speech than by its full permission.

4.53 The only limit to freedom of speech may be on what in general societal feeling is regarded as vulgar and offensive.

4.54 Today's "political correctness"—that is, recognizing some opinions as "correct," i.e., socially acceptable, and others as "incorrect" at the behest of various interest and pressure groups—is a denial of freedom. It is an attempt to introduce the enslavement of minds (or indoctrination) in a new form.

4.6 Freedom of speech and the possibility of choice do not yet cover the full scope of freedom. For human self-realization to take place, it is essential to be able to transform words and intentions into action.

4.61 Freedom must be understood as a necessary and sufficient condition for the effective conduct of any activity. Freedom means access to opportunities for implementing one's own initiative, to the means of action, and to the outcome.

4.611 People who undertake certain activities, as individuals or in groups, as a result of their own choice, who have the appropriate means to achieve their purposes, and who can benefit from the results of their actions, are free.

4.612 Poverty is a denial of freedom. It prevents people from implementing their initiatives and from attaining self-fulfillment.

4.62 Freedom is a powerful force that enables people to carry out activities, and also encourages them to act.

4.621 Freedom is empty or illusory, if, due to the lack of resources for action, intentions cannot be implemented.

4.6211 Without access to capital, it is impossible to develop any project, even with the best ideas of the "industrious and rational" (John Locke).

4.6212 A prerequisite for freedom is the general availability of capital.

4.622 An idea takes on meaning only when it is embodied through active execution.

4.63 The freedom preached about by rebellious and revolutionary movements that challenge tradition is usually an illusory freedom.

4.631 Culture is born of tradition and is based on it. To tradition belongs what has entered from the past into the consciousness of subsequent generations and still exerts an influence on their minds.

4.632 Movements that try to reject tradition are to a society what cancer is to a body.

4.633 An excessive attachment to tradition leads to the stagnation of cultural development and the decay of creative thought; however, the rejection of tradition is worse because it leads to nothingness—it degrades culture and reduces human beings to savagery.

4.7 Freedom appears in the context of the culture of a particular society or group whose members are working together to achieve a particular goal.

4.71 The human being has always been a member of a group or of a larger community. He depends on others because of his need for cooperation.

4.72 Hobbes reduced human beings in the state of nature to isolated and free individuals. However, the individual is always a member of a smaller or a larger community. His freedom and activities are connected to the freedoms and activities of others.

4.721 In the state of nature, as described by Hobbes, there exists constant struggle, fear, and danger of violent death, and, contrary to what he claimed, there is no freedom. Freedom of the individual depends on elimination of threats. Lack of security, individual or collective violence, and chronic poverty are all negations of freedom. In such a social environment, human self-realization is impossible.

4.73 Freedom leads to the improvement of social action, and this depends on human cooperation. Wars, shattering cooperation and separating people into opposing camps, wasting their wealth and destroying their moral principles, are incompatible with freedom and lead to enslavement. Similarly destructive is class conflict or relentless struggle between political parties.

4.8 "Man is not born free, but is born to freedom" (Bronislaw Malinowski).

4.81 Contrary to what is written by Rousseau, human beings are not born free, because they are from birth a part of society and are subject to its rules and other restrictions. Every newborn child is dependent on others, and above all on its immediate family.

4.82 Human beings are born to freedom because they have a capacity for self-fulfillment and achieve self-realization through their own efforts and in the context of the restraints imposed on them by their culture, as long as these restraints are tools of liberty, not instruments of tyranny.

4.821 Freedom is the result of specific cultural conditions that make activities successful and generate benefits. The denial of freedom, incorporated in political and economic restrictions, prevents people from forming intentions, implementing them, and obtaining results.

4.822 We must distinguish between rules and restraints that serve freedom and those that deny freedom.

On the one hand, there are rules that are designed to encourage purposeful and effective action, whose results are shared equitably; on the other hand, there are those rules and organizational principles that, by monopolizing the instruments of violence, wealth, information, and the media, allow groups or individuals to force others to act without permitting them to participate in planning activities or share the results of those activities.

4.823 Freedom, as the possibility of self-realization, depends on factors such as the distribution of wealth, the availability of opportunities to develop individual talent, freedom of movement, vertical social mobility, and the possibility to improve one's social position.

4.83 The whole of history of humankind can be interpreted as the striving of human beings for ever-fuller freedom.

4.831 The scope of freedom, measured by the extent of control people have over the conditions of their lives, increases as culture and civilization develop. The actualization of liberty is served by a well-organized state, which is an important cultural and civilizational factor.

4.832 Freedom is not the absence of constraints but rather the transcending of them. It is associated with an increase in control, efficiency, and power over oneself and one's environment. It means accepting certain restrictions in exchange for effective joint action.

4.833 Both liberty and slavery arise together with culture. The abuse of wealth (the wrong division of material goods), of the law (artificial organizational rules), or of values (inappropriate normative principles and purposes) constitutes a threat to the freedom of individuals, groups, and even entire communities. It destroys civilization from within.

4.834 The progress of humankind, whose determinant is freedom, can occur in every generation, but in each generation there can also be stagnation or even decline.

4.8341 The history of humankind is a history of the rise and fall of civilizations and cultures, states and nations. This history is characterized by ideological disputes and violent changes. It is misleading to represent it in the form of a continuous line in one direction. This line may be interrupted, or may suddenly change direction. It does not represent a rational and necessary progress, as Hegel saw it, nor is it an expression of inevitable political and economic changes that lead us straight to communism, as Marx argued.

4.8342 We can speak of the end of history only if humankind achieves a state of perfection, which is first of all moral perfection, the completeness of virtue, from which humanity is still very far away.

4.84 Freedom is essential for the preservation of civilization and for its development.

4.841 Throughout history we find many forms of enslavement, oppression, discrimination, and domination. Their common feature is the negation of liberty.

4.842 Today the main threats to freedom are the abuse of power and monopoly on the media, along with the lobbies of militarism, religious fanaticism, prostitution, perverted sex, and excessive wealth.

4.843 The abuse of power (political, economic) occurs when individuals or groups of people concentrate power in their hands and use it for their own benefit.

4.844 Monopoly on the media is the concentration of the media in public or private hands, which enables effective indoctrination.

4.845 Lobbies are political pressure groups that, though they do not formally exercise power, can influence government decisions and reap the benefits of this influence.

4.8451 The lobby of militarism mobilizes society for war and profits from war, deriving its revenues from the defense industry. It causes an endless stream of wars.

4.8452 The lobby of religious fanaticism uses violent means, of which the strongest expression is terrorism, to impose on society a radical interpretation of religion in order to gain political power in a given country. It is a grave threat to life, liberty, and reason.

4.8453 The lobby of prostitution is the organized crime network that profits from forcing its victims, mostly women, into prostitution. It subjects these victims to enslavement and reduces them to a means for profit.

4.8454 The lobby of perverted sex undermines traditional marriage between man and woman and leads to the collapse of the institution of the family. In the end, it destroys the whole society.

4.8455 The lobby of excessive wealth rejects all barriers to getting rich and in the pursuit of profit oversteps all political boundaries. It leads to unjustified, large differences in the ownership of property.

4.85 Any enslavement, in which condition a human being becomes the means to an end of another person or group rather than the end of his own development, is a denial of freedom. It forces people into a class that lacks the opportunity to create and develop a culture.

4.851 Human beings who have been turned into subjects or slaves do not realize themselves. They do not take undertake initiatives and do not participate in the distribution of the results of their efforts. As a result, they undergo physical and spiritual degradation.

4.852 Enslavement ensues with the emergence of institutions guided by the notion that people can become means, to be used for another's particular purpose.

4.86 Freedom guarantees that those human qualities that give rise to inspiration, creative ideas, and criticism of the obsolete can flourish. Thanks to freedom, we can gain new knowledge and create new art.

4.87 Freedom depends on the autonomy of the institutions of society (family, local community, school, church). Above all, family life, education, religion, and economic activity must be largely independent from the interference of the state.

4.871 Totalitarianism is opposed to all independence. Its main principle is strict control of all aspects of individual and collective life, and the centralization and unification of all activities.

4.872 Totalitarian rule limits the possibility of individual initiative and social criticism. It replaces spontaneous loyalty to institutions such as the family, church, or local community with loyalty to the central government, imposed from above.

4.88 We can have a culture based on freedom—one that stimulates the development of science, inspires the creation of art, motivates entrepreneurship, deepens morality and spiritual life, gives hope for a better future, and allows human beings to find their own ways of life within the spheres of various opportunities and independent institutions.

4.9 Freedom is defined by cooperation. There is no freedom without solidarity.

5 Solidarity

5   Solidarity is cooperation aimed at achieving the same goals and based on companionship and mutual goodwill.

  5.1   Solidarity implies an equal partnership, which is equal or similar involvement of the participants in joint activities and their equal or similar status as participants.

    5.11   When only some people, who act for the sake of others, are involved in an activity, while others remain passive, then there is no solidarity, but merely aid.

      5.111   Aid to others is a result of compassion—that is, of an active love of one's neighbor; in such a case, help is selfless, but it can be also motivated by specific interests.

        5.1111   Compassion transcends justice and is at the same time its complement. It applies to life situations that the principle of justice does not regulate.

        5.1112   Compassion is revealed in such cases as the act of selflessly helping strangers in need during natural disasters, famine, poverty, accidents, or wars.

    5.12   An expression of solidarity is a self-governing and decentralized society.

  5.2   Solidarity does not preclude the existence of different classes within a society, but it assumes their complementarity, autonomy, and cooperation, instead of their struggle.

    5.21   Freedom, entrepreneurship, and nobility can perfectly complement each other in joint action. Conflict in society appears when freedom changes to usurpation, entrepre-neurship to exploitation, and nobility to arrogance.

5.211 Usurpation is arrogating to oneself benefits or a place in a society for which one does not quailfy, because of a low level of education, lack of virtue, or the presence of other deficiencies.

5.2111 Usurpation is the most serious disease of democracy.

5.2112 The usurper demolishes the spirit of cooperation, which is based on the mutual complementarity of the qualifications of the people who are engaged in a joint undertaking.

5.2113 The political usurper blocks people who are better educated and better suited to holding public office from accessing appropriate positions.

5.2114 Usurpation also occurs in the case of unjustified claims of unqualified employees to manage a company or exorbitant demands on employers by trade unions.

5.212 Exploitation is exclusion from the equitable sharing of benefits in joint action.

5.2121 Exploitation connected to greed and unbridled competition is a common picture in today's business world.

5.2122 Exploitation affects the unity of society, destroys solidarity, creates excessive and unjustified differences in wealth, and represents a great injustice.

5.213 Arrogance (haughtiness) consists in lifting oneself above others.

5.2131 Arrogance of the upper classes is a lack of proper modesty in their relations with members of other classes, an attitude of cynicism, and inaccessibility to people from outside their "proper" society.

5.2132 Like exploitation, arrogance undermines the unity of society and contradicts the spirit of solidarity, which is cooperation.

5.3 Solidarity is destroyed by selfishness and quarrels, and rebuilt by a sense of common identity.

   5.31 One of the biggest internal threats to the state is a power struggle between political parties and the divisions it produces in society.

      5.311 When many competing groups are involved in the ruling of a state, they may cease to be interested in the common good in the heat of political battle, and become focused mainly on their own electoral success and on keeping themselves continuously in power.

         5.3111 The common good serves all members of the political community, and not merely some of its parts.

      5.312 Quarrels among political parties are often artificially produced by highlighting insignificant differences between them and by raising topics that divide society.

         5.3121 Conflicts in the political arena and the consequent creation of social divisions are usually the work of incompetent politicians and reflect the low level of their political culture.

         5.3122 Remedies for quarrels are an ability to compromise and the proper recognition and satisfaction of mutual interests, as long as they are not contrary to the public interest (the common good of the whole society).

   5.32 The practice of social life indicates that cooperation based on the goodwill and companionship of individuals and groups is indispensable for the common good of the whole society and the effective attainment of state goals.

      5.321 The unity and solidarity of society can be achieved by rallying citizens around a political program that is understood by all and that unites rather than divides them.

      5.322 A sense of national and religious identity, which develops in people who are connected by a common history, contributes to their integration and the efficacy of their cooperative efforts.

5.3221 Individuals who, because they lack higher moral values and a specific national or religious identity, are motivated to action only by their own selfish interests will remain in constant conflict with one another—conflict that will split apart the whole of society.

5.3222 The cooperation of state and religion is essential for maintaining a morally healthy, cohesive society, able to defend itself against internal quarrels and threats from the outside world.

5.4 Solidarity is the cooperation of people who are free and benevolent. Its opposite is enmity and the mechanization of humankind based on coercion.

5.41 The philosophy of solidarity has deep roots in Christian thought, commanding people to love their neighbors, and this means treating them as ends, not as means to an end.

5.411 People who treat each other with love, as ends in themselves, recognize their mutual autonomy. Such people are free.

5.412 All forms of servitude, exploitation, and slavery treat others as means to an end.

5.413 Christianity, erecting a civilization of love, is a great and difficult task, and continues to be the still incomplete journey of humanity toward ever-greater moral perfection. This journey is also a road to freedom.

5.4131 Christianity as a journey toward ever-greater moral perfection is not merely Christianity as a specific religion or a particular church, but as a universal task for all humankind.

5.4132 All religions, all ideologies of human brotherhood, all nations, and all individual persons are invited on the journey together toward moral perfection,

5.4133 Perfection is expressed in harmony—in the beauty that can be found in nature, art, and human conduct. Today's world is a domain of turbulence and dissonance. There is still much to do on the road toward the moral perfection of humanity.

5.4134 The first step toward moral perfection is the moral improvement of individual and public life, based on the fundamental principle of natural law, which is doing no harm to others.

5.4135 Moral perfection manifests itself in cooperation—in solidarity among people in a given society, among nations, and among all humanity.

5.42 The philosophy of the enemy, which can be found both in Marxism and in the philosophy of Carl Schmitt, as well as in twentieth-century political realism and in many streams of today's critical and postmodern philosophy, divides humanity into proletarians and capitalists, friends and foes, democrats and non-democrats, us and them, women and men—all remaining in a constant state of hostility and conflict with one another. And because none of these groups can achieve a permanent victory over the one opposing it, the conflict lasts forever.

5.421 The philosophy of the enemy, which is based on false assumptions and dogmas concerning human nature, transforms people into enemies.

5.4211 Enmity is not innate to human beings, but it can be learned.

5.4212 War is not caused by human nature. Neither aggression, nor belligerence, nor enmity, nor hatred can be considered a primary biological impulse of human beings.

5.4213 Enmity and belligerence are not the basic behavior of human beings, but rather are derivative and culturally shaped. They can occur when, because of intervention by other individuals, human beings are threatened in their ability to meet their primary biological needs (for food, sex, security), or when the fulfillment of their culturally determined needs (for wealth, social position) is disrupted.

5.42131 At the root of enmity and hatred, there may always be found particular interests of individuals or groups.

5.4214 Culture in its various forms defines our behavior. Since our behavior is subject to cultural recasting, that which will tend to eliminate enmity and hatred, rather than that which will fuel it, should become the content of mass media coverage and the educational process.

5.4215 Enmity can be artificially produced, as well as prevented. By the employment of such cultural means as propaganda and indoctrination, the friendship of the recent past can change into today's hatred; but by the same token, the target of yesterday's hostility can quickly become a partner in a new pact.

5.4216 Collective hatred and the incitement of enmity are the result of activities carried out by the media. In today's world there is an artificial fabrication of fear and hate, used to create enemies and justify military spending. The gainers are, first of all, the interest groups that profit from the defense industry.

5.422 The philosophy of the enemy leads humanity to continuous revolution and turmoil, in which the most important thing is not determining who is at odds with whom, because ideologies and actors are constantly changing, but ensuring that the conflict lasts forever.

5.4221 The purpose of the game is to have hostility engulf all, setting each against the other, with a goal of chaos and revolution.

5.4222 In political practice, the philosophy of the enemy is also expressed in the inability, or even the lack of a sincere desire, to resolve conflicts, both internal and international (with such conflicts continuing for years and becoming ever more bitter), as well as in the highly turbulent and unstable nature of politics and public life today.

5.4223 For a proper assessment of any political situation, we should be able to recognize the interests of the parties involved and to distinguish real threats from those induced artificially.

5.423 The purpose of cultures that are based on the philosophy of solidarity and collegial cooperation is the avoidance of crises and, when they occur, their resolution; the purpose of cultures based on the philosophy of the enemy and enmity is causing crises and using them as a means to an end—gaining power.

5.4231 In a chaotic situation, the principal fomenters of disturbance always obtain the leading positions for themselves.

5.4232 In an ideological struggle against human solidarity, tradition and religion come under attack.

5.4233 The weaker the ties of common culture and identity binding people together, the greater the opportunity for their misunderstanding and mutual opposition, leading to hostility.

5.424 When humanity is influenced by the philosophy of the enemy, when enmity and hatred become increasingly prevailing feelings—when, at the expense of the development of many other areas of life, it constructs a huge war machine, perfects its system of espionage, and develops special forces—then humanity, in this situation, is moving on a direct road to annihilation.

5.425 Identifying the philosophy of the enemy with the whole of Western European civilization is a major misunderstanding, and is especially hurtful for Christians. The philosophy of the enemy, which is the essence of Militarism, is directed against Western Europe's traditional civilization, which is the classical-Christian civilization.

5.4251 Militarism has led to the most radical cultural revolution in the history of humankind. It depicts other human beings as the enemy and changes nations and their resources from instruments of peaceful cooperation to instruments of violence.

5.4252 Militarism, like its sibling, twentieth-century political realism, rejects the possibility of cooperation between people and introduces the concept of the struggle for power as a primary motivation for human behavior.

5.4253 By means of indoctrination, slander, and lies, Militarism mobilizes a society for the purpose of war. It affects not only the state's foreign policy, but also its educational system, legal system, economy, science, and art.

5.4254 The ultimate goal of Militarism is the domination of the world by one nation (or one culture) and the permanent reshaping of humanity by means of the ideology of that nation (or culture).

5.4255 Militarism is the negation of the ideals of Christianity (and, more broadly, those of Classicism). It is a form of totalitarianism and a flight from freedom. It changes a community of free individuals into a human machine—a blind instrument of power and a means for a particular purpose: domination.

5.4256 The recent and infamous fruits of Militarism have been Nazism and Stalinism. It still remains a great threat to humankind.

5.43 Byzantism eliminates freedom by means of its all-powerful bureaucracy and its extended mechanism of control over all aspects of human existence.

5.431 Like Militarism, Byzantism rejects the ideal of the peaceful cooperation of free people embedded in a common culture—the ideal derived from Classicism.

5.432 Byzantism replaces all other sources of cultural inspiration (such as influence of the family, independent institutions, and religion) by laws imposed from the top. It places the institution of the state above all others. It is an attempt by the state to dominate other institutions and replace their functions with prescriptive control. It extends its control to the realms of family relationships, education, and the economy.

5.4321 The dominant contemporary trend related to the influence of Byzantism is the belief in the effectiveness of artificially and arbitrarily enacted laws. As a result, laws penetrate into every corner of life. However, artificial rules—the laws of tyranny—are either ineffective or destructive to the basic institutions of social life.

5.4322 Rules that have been established by tradition, and that arise from the experience of human cooperation, serve freedom. Such rules or laws of liberty may result in highly disciplined actions, for the very reason that they are not artificial rules and do not require the involvement of significant means of coercion.

5.4323 Artificial rules are arbitrarily imposed laws that are in conflict with the experience of individuals. For their implementation, it is necessary to use indoctrination and violence.

5.433 Byzantism is the mechanization and standardization of humanity.

    5.4331 The standardization of humanity on the basis of universal and detailed rules for all cannot be reconciled with the existence and progress of culture. Byzantism, which can sometimes inspire us with admiration for the immensity of its constructions, in reality brings culture to a standstill.

    5.4332 The mechanization of human relationships through bureaucratic intervention, indoctrination, and the apparatus of coercion cannot replace the relationships between husband and wife, or parents and children, the relations among colleagues, or the solidarity of people who work together. Such relationships have been culturally formed during a long historical process.

    5.4333 Virtues such as perseverance and courage, charity and wisdom cannot be imposed by law or engendered by coercion.

5.434 The cultural mission of Byzantism is sameness and uniformity, because this is how Byzantism understands unity. If Byzantism preaches diversity, it is only illusory. Through legislation and indoctrination that permeate all aspects of private life—home, school, business, and worship—Byzantism abolishes all autonomy in society.

    5.4341 In early modernity the fanatical quest for uniformity was a source of religious wars in Western Europe, and its clear expression was the rule established in Augsburg in 1555, *cuius regio, eius religio* (whose authority, his religion), according to which the religion obligatory in the country would depend on the religion of the ruler.

5.435 As a form of totalitarianism, Byzantism destroys the normal, traditional way of life, and in the end the nation itself. It replaces this with a human machine, with an artificially created society.

5.436 The essence of Byzantism is centralism and uniformity; that of Classicism, autonomy and diversity.

    5.4361 To protect a creative culture, one should unite—but not unify—to create unity in diversity.

5.437 Byzantism can refer to oriental civilization, which took shape in ancient Persia, and then began to influence the Roman Empire. It flourished in Byzantium. Its influence could later be noted in Europe, notably but no means solely in Russia. Byzantism in fact had a significant impact on the culture of Germany and influenced the culture of France, especially during the period of absolutism.

    5.4371 Thomas Hobbes, often considered a founder of modern political philosophy, was influenced by French legalists. He was a supporter of absolutism and attempted to introduce Byzantism into England. Evidences of Hobbes's Byzantism are his concept of an unlimited and undivided power, and his idea of freedom. In *Leviathan* he writes, "There is written on the turrets of the city Luca in great characters at this day, the word LIBERTAS; yet no man can thence inferre that a particular man has more Libertie, or Immunitie from the service of the Commonwealth there, than in Constantinople." Hobbes, for whom freedom is the absence of restraint and the lack of limitations, and for whom law is coercion, could not distinguish republican liberty from oriental bondage.

    5.4372 The most notable creation of Byzantism to be seen today is (probably contrary to the expectations of its founders) the European Union. The European Union has typical

Byzantine features, such as an extensive bureaucracy and a bureaucratic centralism, which has produced, among other things, a centralized fiscal and economic policy. Moreover, it demonstrates a Byzantine belief that everything can be achieved mechanically by law and a corresponding willingness to make uniform all aspects of life and to encroach in any and every area, including sexual life, the family, and education. It is an attempt to construct a new, artificial European identity that results in the destruction of national cultures.

5.4373 Replacing the creative civic spirit arising from liberty and solidarity with mechanized human relationships that are controlled centrally, from above, is contrary to Classicism and introduces into Europe a grave civilizational conflict.

5.4374 Byzantism has always led to civilizational stagnation, and so it is with the European Union. Instead of making Europe into a competitive economic power, the Union has led to economic crisis and massive unemployment.

5.4375 The European Union has its ideologues, who stubbornly pursue the agenda to deepen the Union; that is, they aim at a greater level of integration, which would ultimately involve the loss of autonomy of its member states.

5.4376 Instead of deepening the Union, we should rather return to the earlier concept of the European Community and give member states more independence.

5.4377 In order to survive, the European Union must accept the ideas of autonomy and diversity, and, first and foremost, leave outside its political control the oldest institution of humanity, which is the family, as well as the spheres of morality and national traditions.

5.43771 The European Union would do better with less bureaucracy and more poetry.

5.5 Solidarity is based on individuals and institutions joined by bonds of cooperation, the most fundamental institution among these being the family.

5.51 The family is a universal institution of humanity, and its oldest.

5.511 The traditional family—a unit composed of a man, the father, and a woman, the mother, together with their children—can be found in all cultures, from the earliest times to today.

5.5111 The family fulfills two main functions: ensuring the continuity of the human race and enabling the continuity of culture.

5.5112 The family regulates relations between the sexes, stimulates procreation, educates new generations, and maintains family and national traditions.

5.5113 The effective operation of the family is based on respect for its rules (sexual limits and liberties, the division of labor between husband and wife, the duty of older members of family to take care of the younger and provide for their education, the obedience of children to parents).

5.512 The family begins with marriage.

5.5121 The mutual love of the spouses is the bond of family life.

5.5122 Love, faithfulness, commitment to each other, mutual assistance, and mutual respect are the basic conditions for marital happiness.

5.5123 Marriage without children is not yet a proper family.

5.5124 The aim of marriage is children.

5.513 The family is not limited to the father, mother, and their children, but includes all those who are joined by ties of kinship, both the living and those who have left this world.

    5.5131 The dead must remain in our memories. Their deeds, if noble, influence the living by providing a good example and thereby improving them; if erroneous, serve as a warning and educate them to do better.

5.52 The family should always be protected from the breach of its autonomy by the state.

    5.521 Along with the development of the modern state, there has been a tendency to restrict the autonomous role of the family through subjection to the state authority.

        5.5211 Education, law, and the economy are separated more and more from the sphere of traditional institutions—the family and the local community—and come increasingly under the control of new institutions: schools, courts, and workplaces.

        5.5212 Along with the advancement of postmodernism, there occurs the redefinition of the family as a partnership—an artificial invention, which does not serve procreation and is not based on the relationship between a man and a woman.

    5.522 State bureaucrats are today immersed in a frenzy of unjustified reformism. It is dangerous to manipulate the most powerful human impulse, sex, and to interfere with the rules and customs that have grown up around it over the course of human biological and social development.

    5.523 If we destroy the traditional institution of the family, the annihilation of reproduction, kinship systems, and education will follow. In this way, society will condemn itself to self-destruction.

5.53 In a society based on solidarity, families and other institutions endowed with adequate autonomy work together.

5.6 The widest range of solidarity is global solidarity. It is expressed in the cooperation of people from around the world.

5.61 In view of the cultural and civilizational differences between people, their cooperation on a global scale is very difficult, but possible. It increases with the development of global consciousness.

    5.611 The development of global consciousness is stimulated by the development of advanced means of transportation and communication, especially the Internet.

    5.612 Global consciousness is based on the understanding that despite their differences, all people have common needs and interests, and their lives in this condition of globalization are mutually dependent.

        5.6121 There are certain minimum conditions required for life. All people need clean air and water, appropriate clothing, and a warm, dry place to live. They need to eat and reproduce for their own survival and that of their species. They also need care and education during their youth and protection against diseases and other dangers.

        5.6122 Regardless of existing material, cultural, and political differences among human beings, the contemporary world imposes on them a number of common interests. Motivated by self-interest, people must engage in international trade, take care of their natural environment, comply with the rules of hygiene, and follow various customs and practices of a universally beneficial nature.

5.62 Global solidarity establishes cooperation among people on the basis of the recognition of their common needs and interests, regardless of their differences.

    5.621 Every human being has a natural desire to live a happy life; that is, a safe and prosperous life that allows for self-realization.

    5.622 Needs related to food, shelter, family, and safety are universal, arising from human life itself.

5.6221 It is true that some people may forsake family and safety, and embrace solitude, adventure, and risk to reach their goals. Solitude, adventure, and risk can indeed become a private way of life for some people, but a sustainable life cannot be built on them.

5.6222 The same applies to war. War for the purposes of conquest can be a way of life, or a part of life, and yet we cannot build a fulfilling communal life on this basis. The normal process of human development and self-realization requires peace.

5.6223 Even the most warlike peoples of the past did not live only for war. To survive as a group, they first had to solve their basic life problems, that is, how to reproduce, educate new generations, and procure for themselves the goods needed to live.

5.6224 For its preservation, human life in a community requires cooperation and the continuity of generations.

5.623 The development of individuals requires the presence of not only the basic necessities of life, such as food, shelter, family, and safety, but also liberty and respect.

5.6231 Individuals cannot fully develop without freedom. They also cannot be fully happy in life without respect and recognition, as well as kindness and friendship, from others.

5.6232 Enmity, injustice, discourtesy, disrespect, hatred, and violence on the part of others, along with the impact of ideas that are detrimental to cooperation, reduce the chances of improving interpersonal relationships and ensuring the correct development of personalities.

5.6233 A policy toward others based on naked force cannot be effective.

5.63 Human beings are divided by cultures, civilizations, religions, ideologies, nationalities, and their particular interests, yet they can still find common ground. What unites all of us without exception is our basic needs, whose satisfaction is necessary to human life.

    5.631 Let us ask if there is anything that we all share. That thing is life itself. Life is the central concept, around which humanity can unite.

    5.632 Some human needs can be considered indispensable, not only for a simple life, but also for a fulfilled and happy life.

    5.633 Global solidarity depends on the recognition of life as the common ground on which all human beings, despite their differences, can meet.

        5.6331 Whether global solidarity could be established on the basis of various existing nongovernmental organizations (NGOs) that share a similar program and could become something like an umbrella organization for them, or whether it would be a completely new establishment, are purely technical questions.

        5.6332 The foundation of global solidarity is the understanding of needs that are common to all human beings, together with our readiness to cooperate.

5.64 Global solidarity results from the existence of brotherhood among people and is an expression of unity arising from diversity.

    5.641 Human brotherhood presupposes empathy, partnership, and cooperation.

        5.6411 Cosmopolitanism, a feeling of kinship that individuals have with the whole of humanity, does not negate their emotional ties with their own country, but is an expression of a broader, nonparochial view of the surrounding reality. It expresses the idea that because of our common humanity, we have moral obligations not only to our family members and fellow citizens, but also to all people.

5.6412 Cosmopolitan responsibility means an obligation to protect from wrong those upon whom it is being inflicted, no matter where they live and who they are, and to give value to each human being, irrespective of whether or not he or she belongs to our own political community.

5.6413 Although the bonds of brotherhood unite us with all people, we should be dedicated to our kinfolk in a special way. In the order of moral obligation, our family and our country come first; then comes the cosmopolitan responsibility for all human beings.

5.642 Those who negate brotherhood among human beings are the lobbies of militarism, prostitution, religious fanaticism, perverted sex, and excessive wealth.

5.6421 The lobbies of militarism, prostitution, religious fanaticism, perverted sex, and excessive wealth, all of which increase the strength of their impact on society under conditions of globalization, have one thing in common: they destroy the free development of human beings and turn people into the means they use to achieve their own ends.

5.6422 Globalization means interdependence. The whole world is now transformed into a single market that has been penetrated by multinational corporations and is united by the mutual dependencies of one state on the others and of all states on one another.

5.6423 Connected to globalization are both benefits resulting from human cooperation and new risks related to environmental pollution, economic exploitation, poverty, terrorism, and cross-border crime.

5.65 Global solidarity arises when human beings become conscious of their mutual dependence in today's world and when they have a common understanding of what is right for life.

    5.651 Global solidarity is based on the righteousness of life.

    5.652 Positive world transformation is based on the assumption that conflict is an important part of life, but does not constitute its essence, and that social progress and the enhancement of life are possible. On the practical side, world transformation requires that we try to minimize conflict and avert the danger of war, and protect life and allow life to flourish.

5.7 An integral part of any cooperation is authority (government).

    5.71 The government fulfills a leadership function in society.

        5.711 The existence of government is natural. There cannot be life in a society without leadership.

        5.712 Cooperation involves specialization and a division of labor. On these depend the prosperity of a society and its civilizational progress.

            5.7121 In each group there are those who make decisions, give commands, oversee their execution, and thus direct the group; there are also those who are guided by them.

        5.713 The function of government is not only that of a night watchman, but also that of an organizer of social life.

            5.7131 As part of its function, government protects society against internal and external dangers and organizes it for cooperation within the framework of an existing legal order.

            5.7132 Beyond ensuring the security of citizens, the basic function of government is to balance individual and group interests, to define the possibilities of self-realization for all, and to prevent the monopoly of any aspect of social life by any person, group, or class.

5.7133 In cases when, relying on self-government, society organizes itself, the best organizational role government can play is that of a coordinator.

5.72 Authority is the power of making decisions, controlling the means for their execution, and allocating the outcomes, as well as the privilege of holding a certain status in the society.

5.721 An authority that imposes an appropriate discipline upon individuals is required in any educational process and for any successful joint action.

5.7211 Discipline is a prerequisite for success. No culture can develop without the element of discipline that is introduced by obedience and sanctioned by force.

5.7212 Even when people are subject to a certain discipline, they remain free, as long as this discipline is essential for the enactment of intentions resulting from their own free choice.

5.7213 Proper discipline is a civilizational factor and an essential feature of human cooperation. Its direct contradiction is the authoritarian discipline that is imposed on people from above and treats them only as passive instruments of action, as means for a particular purpose.

5.73 One needs to distinguish between authorities that subject people to a proper discipline, which is needed for effective cooperation and the proper functioning of society in the condition of freedom, and authorities that abuse their power and represent a denial of freedom.

5.731 The abuse of political power always occurs where the purpose of action is imposed by top-down command or enforced by indoctrination, where the means of action are controlled from above, and where the outcomes of action are not equitably distributed, but instead benefit primarily those who are in power.

5.7311 An authority becomes oppressive when, by using means of coercion, it obtains benefits for certain individuals or groups at the expense of others.

5.732 The abuse of power by certain individuals or groups occurs in defective political regimes, such as tyranny, oligarchy, and populist and totalitarian democracy.

5.7321 Class rule, exercised in the interest of a ruling class, is a perversion of government, and can be found only in defective political regimes.

5.7322 Defective political regimes are associated with centralism.

5.74 The negation of cooperation is a struggle for power.

5.741 The struggle for power escalates in the case of weak governments and corrupted societies.

5.7411 Corruption in society is related to moral decline and the fading of virtue among citizens, and is articulated in their egoism, quarrels, and envy.

5.7412 In a morally healthy society, one gains political power, as well as fame and glory, through serving society by means of deeds and wisdom; in a morally corrupted one, through providing benefits to private individuals—that is, through corruption.

5.7413 In a corrupted society, public positions are obtained not by those who because of their personal qualifications deserve them, but by those who are better able to flatter the masses and usurp dominion for themselves. In such a society, politicians gain supporters and coalition partners by means of corruption.

5.7414 "What the lord does, the many do after him" (Lorenzo the Magnificent). Corruption of those in authority plunges the whole of society into corruption.

5.8 The natural tendency of human beings that follows from their social character is to cooperate. Moral corruption and cultural and civilizational differences among people hinder cooperation and change brotherhood into enmity.

    5.81 The presence of virtues in society is necessary for effective cooperation aimed at realizing common goals and maintaining a strong, well-organized state.

    5.82 Citizens' nobility comprises the civic virtues: courage, honesty, respect for the law, diligence, and, above all, love of freedom and of one's country.

        5.821 A nation that loses its nobility goes into decline, experiences internal quarrels, becomes divided, and turns into a passive, lifeless collection of people who can be easily manipulated and enslaved.

    5.83 No society can be happy without nobility.

        5.831 Without this value—without nobility—societies undergo a process of moral degradation and states cannot be well governed.

5.9 There is no liberty without solidarity; there is no solidarity without nobility.

6 Sophocracy

6 Sophocracy is ennobled democracy.

  6.1 The basic feature of democracy is freedom.

    6.11 The essence of freedom in democracy is autonomy; that is, an area given to citizens within which they can shape their own lives as individuals and as groups: the family, the community, the ethnic group, the religious group, the whole of society.

      6.111 Democracy consists of a number of autonomous but related and cooperating institutions. The salient characteristics of democracy are the separation of religious institutions and the institution of the state, the independence of scientific and economic organizations, the self-government of territorial units, and local autonomy.

    6.12 Free elections and a multiplicity of political parties are a necessary condition of modern democracy, but are not its sufficient condition, which is freedom. Without freedom in the form of the autonomy of individuals, groups, and institutions, a "democracy" is only an ostensible democracy.

      6.121 When democracy does not ensure the autonomy of individuals and groups, it takes the form of tyranny and becomes its own negation. It becomes democracy in name only.

        6.1211 Totalitarian democracy, in which there is a lack of freedom, is a form of tyranny. Such a democracy is not only a paradox, but also a common phenomenon.

6.122 Democratic revolutions are often illusory. Their effect is a change of the form of government to a multiparty system, but they do not bring real freedom, which comprises freedom of expression, conscience, and association, and the autonomy of individuals and groups. In many cases, these revolutions do not give security or prosperity to citizens, nor do they provide other conditions for the development of culture.

6.1221 Chronic poverty, economic disarray, and insecurity are the antithesis of freedom and democracy.

6.2 Democracy is a political system based on self-government.

6.21 Self-government means governing oneself—that is, self-determination, and this is synonymous with freedom.

6.22 In the case of direct democracy, citizens themselves govern their country, participating in conventions and meetings, making decisions, and enacting laws.

6.221 In the case of representative democracy, they do this through their own, freely elected representatives.

6.2211 Free elections are those in which all free citizens have the right to participate—to choose their representatives and to be elected.

6.2212 A free citizen is one who has the power to decide about his or her own life—that is, a person who has reached the age of maturity, has full mental powers, and has not entered into conflict with the law and so remains free.

6.2213 Although students and the unemployed may disagree with this thesis, we can also reasonably expect of free citizens that they are able to earn their living and pay taxes.

6.23 The organization of government in the form of self-government does not apply only in relation to the central state authority, but also to provincial and local authorities at various levels.

6.231 The self-government of provincial and local administrations means their autonomy in relation to the central state government with respect to some of the tasks they perform.

6.232 Based on the principle of the self-government, democracy provides autonomy for the organized cooperation of citizens in achieving common goals.

6.3 Democracy is the rule of citizens.

6.31 The definition of democracy as "government of the people, exercised by the people, for the people" is misleading if by "the people" we understand only the poorer and less-educated part of society, rather than the whole of society, composed of all citizens.

6.311 If democracy were the government of poorer and less-educated people, trying to deprive the rich of their property and assign all members of society to a single material and intellectual level, then it would deserve no more than to be called a "populist democracy" or a "people's democracy," and as such it would be classified as a defective political regime.

6.32 Democracy, as a correct political regime, is the "government of citizens, (exercised) by citizens, for citizens."

6.321 Citizens' governance—self-government—is the essence of democracy.

6.322 The government *of* citizens means their broad participation in government at the local, provincial, and national levels.

6.3221 The broad participation of citizens in government is associated with their rotation. Politicians in a democracy cannot always be the same small group of people.

6.323 Government *for* citizens means that government is aimed at the common good, and no citizen should be excluded from the benefits of living in society.

6.3231 Any exclusion introduces into society an element of tyranny and is contrary to freedom, which is a fundamental feature of democracy.

6.3232 Democracy is not for just "the people," or just "the rich," or just for the politicians, media celebrities, large corporations, or the state bureaucracy; it is for all citizens and cannot omit anyone, particularly persons of noble character.

6.4 Proper democracy, as opposed to flawed democracy, which is a populist or a totalitarian democracy, is one of the correct political regimes.

6.41 In addition to proper democracy, which in the Aristotelian classification of regimes is called *polity*, the correct political regimes typically include monarchy and aristocracy.

6.42 In a proper democracy, there are a multiplicity of groups, social classes, and sometimes even different cultures. Despite the differences among them, they are united by cooperation and one main purpose, which is the common good.

6.43 Proper democracy gives citizens, first, freedom to formulate intentions and form opinions, that is, freedom of speech and of conscience; second, freedom of action, that is, freedom of association, of business activity, and of participation in political life; and third, freedom of outcomes, that is, freedom to enjoy the fruits of their work and activities.

6.44 The negations of the idea of proper democracy include: a vast bureaucracy that tries to administer all aspects of human life; class rule, which can be found in defective political regimes; quarrels within society that are stimulated by the struggle of political parties; the monopolization of economic and political life by pressure groups; and indoctrination or any other apparatus of social control and coercion, be it secret or overt.

6.441 As a regime of liberty, democracy rules out monopolies on wealth, media, and information, as well as other forms of exploitation and social exclusion. Its freedom, the essence of which is autonomy and self-government, is the possibility of self-realization on the part of individuals, groups, and the whole society.

6.442 In a proper democracy, we should always strive to limit overreaching administration, excessive wealth, and the influence of pressure groups.

    6.4421 Overreaching administration is associated with a vast bureaucracy.

    6.4422 Bureaucracy bases its actions on specific rules and regulations that are laid down by senior officials, and hence it discourages any initiative.

6.5 Proper democracy, like other correct political regimes, implements principles of justice.

  6.51 Justice is the foundation of a good social order.

  6.52 The principle of justice in a democracy is not sameness or equalization, because this negates freedom.

    6.521 Equality in society is derived from the principle of freedom and cannot contradict it.

    6.522 The consequences of freedom as the possibility of self-realization are equality of opportunity and equality in assessment, that is, impartiality; however, equality as sameness is its contradiction.

    6.523 Equality as sameness can only be achieved by coercion. In this way, human communities are tyrannized and mechanized.

    6.524 The existence of a multiplicity and diversity of influences on individuals prevents their indoctrination and mental enslavement. This multiplicity and diversity depends on the existence of independent institutions, namely those that, although linked with one another, have a significant degree of autonomy.

  6.53 Justice in a state is a result of the skillful organization of diversity.

    6.531 Justice, as the foundation of social order in a democracy, is based on the fact of human diversity and, at the same time, of equality.

    6.532 Society consists of various groups and social classes, and sometimes also different cultures that represent different values and interests; in accordance with the principle of freedom, each of them has the right to self-realization, of which the limit can only be the self-realization of others.

6.54 The idea of justice is to create conditions for harmonious self-realization; that is, justice reconciles and harmonizes different values and different individual and group interests.

    6.541 The purpose of justice is the achievement of harmonious cooperation between different individuals, groups, and classes, and diverse cultures.

6.55 The primary tasks of a democratic government as a guarantor of justice are balancing group interests, preventing monopolization in any area of life by pressure groups, and leading society to cooperation.

6.56 The principle of justice is the right of everyone to what he or she legitimately deserves.

    6.561 The right of persons or groups to what they legitimately deserve cannot undermine the rights of other persons or groups.

    6.562 Justice in a state is not identical with the interest of any particular person, group, or class, but must always refer to the common good of society.

    6.563 The principle of justice implemented in the form of laws and customs, provides a political community with a sense of unity, and is a prerequisite of its prosperity and strength.

6.57 Natural law and the common good of society are the ultimate indicators of what is just in a state, and what is not.

6.6 Sophocracy—democracy proper and ennobled—combines within itself freedom and wisdom.

    6.61 Wisdom and, more broadly, talent—the special ability of particular individuals and groups to perform given tasks—is an element of culture and has an important social function.

    6.611 While, in conjunction with the principle of freedom as the possibility of self-realization, all citizens in a democracy are entitled to equal access to education and knowledge, the performance of specific tasks belongs to those who are best suited.

6.612 Distribution of jobs according to race, nationality, social status, gender, or sexual orientation, with which we are dealing in the case of affirmative action or other forms of positive discrimination, is contrary to the natural distribution of tasks according to ability, and is unfair because it leads to the exclusion from action of more talented persons and reduces the chances for effective cooperation.

    6.6121 Affirmative action policies that aim to equalize opportunities and privileges for groups that were allegedly discriminated against in the past are artificial policies, often introducing cultural confusion and promoting merely ostensible justice.

    6.6122 Something can never be right if it benefits some and harms others.

6.62 One of the most difficult and most responsible assignments is to govern the state.

    6.621 The art of government requires people best suited to this task: leaders with the appropriate skills, knowledge, and morality.

        6.6211 Leaders of countries should be wise people: comprehensively educated, endowed with many skills and considerable life experience, and specially equipped for the function of leadership.

        6.6212 Additional requirements for those in positions of power are a sense of tradition and of relationship with their own people, along with nobility, expressed in acting for the sake of the common good.

6.63 The presence of virtues in the human being, combined with education and experience, is the greatest entitlement to rule.

    6.631 The fundamental virtue of state leaders is wisdom. It is expressed in prudence and an ability to make the best possible choices. However, it goes deeper, to include complete knowledge.

6.6311 The knowledge that is necessary to govern encompasses not only the knowledge of a number of areas, including security, foreign policy, strategy, and economics, but also the in-depth knowledge of the nature and highest goals of human beings, the source of which is philosophy and religion.

6.64 Plato was right when he wrote: "The human race will have no respite from evils until those who are really philosophers [lovers of wisdom] acquire political power or until, through some divine dispensation, those who rule and have political authority in the cities become real philosophers."

6.641 Al-Farabi was also right when he stated, "If a sage, who can bring wisdom to the government, will not come, after some time the state shall inevitably perish."

6.6411 Such a sage should have a sharp and penetrating mind, love science, truth, and justice, be magnanimous and inclined to noble things, be able to express himself beautifully, and "be assertive, courageous, enterprising, and know no fear or weakness of spirit in these matters, which he considers as his responsibility" (Al-Farabi).

6.6412 And if there is no one human being who concentrates in himself or herself all these qualities and all of the necessary knowledge, a few individuals (or even more) who together combine these qualities would also suffice. The most important thing is that they should actually stand at the head of the state.

6.65 Usurpation—people with no qualifications running for high government offices—is the greatest disease of democracy.

6.66 In a society where there is no room for wisdom and nobility, political power is gained by the worst.

6.661 Without this virtue, without nobility, individual and group egoism emerges; a parasitic elite is born.

6.662 The parasitic elite is composed of individuals who, while occupying influential political positions, suppress the public interest in favor of their own interests.

6.663 If politics is subordinated to the particular interests of those who are in power or is subject to the influences of the lobby of militarism and other powerful political pressure groups who focus on their own benefits, then even the potentially best regime, which is democracy, changes into a defective regime.

6.67 Democracy devoid of wisdom becomes blind. Blindness then does not allow democracy to see that in such case, it turns from the rule of freedom into tyranny.

6.7 At the basis of sophocracy, proper democracy, there is wisdom, freedom, and nobility.

6.71 Nobility is a complete virtue. The human being who personifies nobility is a noble person.

6.711 Virtues are not innate in human beings, but can be developed.

6.712 Because of the culture they create, a part of which is education, human beings can transform their desires and instinctive reactions into the kind of behavior that is modified by the cultural values that are virtues.

6.713 There are as many virtues as there are actions specific to human beings, for every action has its virtue.

6.714 In order for their actions to be morally best, people should develop complete virtue—a set of complementary positive qualities, such as benevolence, initiative, courage, diligence, prudence, modesty, justice (righteousness), moderation, cooperation, and determination.

6.72 The distinguishing traits of noble persons are not harming others and being guided by the common good, even if harm to others would bring them certain benefits. This is due to their righteousness—that is, sense of justice.

6.721 "For the noble person, character is integrity, actions are correctness, and attitude is modesty" (Confucius).

6.722 "An upright person is one who helps all whom he can and harms nobody, unless provoked by wrong" (Cicero).

6.73 In every society, complete virtue, consisting of intelligence, good manners, and high moral values, is, like good education and good taste, the distinguishing feature of a minority. This minority, characterized by its noble qualities, can be called the elite of honor and merit. It is sometimes described as "the salt of the nation."

6.731 The elite of honor and merit is the minority group, composed of people who are noble, resourceful, and educated, and who in every generation contribute to the maintenance and development of various aspects of culture; and if these people are replaced by others who are less diligent and less talented, culture declines.

6.732 We can observe a continuous rises and falls of cultures. Their fate depends primarily on the quality of the available human resources involved in their preservation; on individual talent, initiative, diligence, courage, wisdom, and integrity.

6.74 The function of wisdom in society is competent governance; the function of nobility is harmonious cooperation.

6.741 A noble and educated minority, the elite of honor and merit, is the basis for the civilizational development of any society.

6.7411 Without a proper elite, the political community, torn apart by internal rifts and political power struggles, and dominated by a parasitic elite, will not be a real community, nor will it be well governed.

6.75 Governing the state is an operation too complex for a mediocre mind.

6.751 The opinion that someone who was weak at school can suddenly become a great politician is mistaken. Politics, the art of governing, is highly sophisticated; therefore, it needs people who are well educated and wise. So we must find a place in politics for high-achieving students.

6.752 Someone who lacks a solid education, but by chance learns something about a particular topic and at times says something clever, is not a wise person, but only a "shrewd bumpkin."

6.753 When mediocre people hold political power, not only do they not produce anything good, they usually do much damage.

6.7531 Aware of their mediocrity, yet wanting to distinguish themselves and make their mark in some way, they undertake reforms that are no more than superficial.

6.754 Those superficial reforms that look best on paper usually expose the state to unnecessary costs and not only do not improve anything, but in fact worsen the organization of society.

6.755 Superficial reforms often occur in democracy and are, after usurpation and political inanity, its third greatest disease.

6.76 The disharmony that we can see in the political life of many countries and in international politics is the result of a deficit of wisdom and nobility among politicians.

6.761 Given today's technological advancement and the mutual interdependence among states consequent to globalization, the current disharmony in the world is a serious threat to the continued existence of all humankind.

6.762 "When weapons and ignorance come together, tyrants arise to devastate the world with their cruelty" (Rumi).

6.77 To repair the world in its present, increasingly deteriorating condition, mediocre people are no longer good enough; people who are wise and noble are needed.

6.771 The greater the number of noble people in a society, the greater its health and resistance to the vicissitudes of life.

6.78 If from the principle of freedom in a democracy equal opportunities for all are derived, so from individuals' wisdom and nobility come their roles in the government of the state and their positions in society.

6.781 In a correct political regime, the determination of what one deserves, and thus the role of an individual or a group in society, can be made only with respect to the common good; that is, with respect to what is beneficial for the whole society.

6.7811 The just distribution of roles and obligations in any political community is one that contributes to effective cooperation and the achievement of the common good, and not to that community's division into rival political parties or other groups, whose principal goal is their own benefit.

6.782 Politics is the ability to actualize a good life for a society, and so those who are guided by the common good and can contribute most to their country's prosperity should be in government.

6.79 Because of their intellectual and moral qualities, people who are wise and noble should have top positions in society and leading roles in the state.

6.791 The place of wisdom and nobility in politics should be ensured by an appropriate electoral law that enables the selection of the best individuals for office, based on their education and personal qualification, rather than one that serves political parties in their struggle for power.

6.792 Persons selected for their noble qualities should serve in the Senate and other chambers of the Parliament.

6.7921 The Senate, or upper chamber, is an indispensable element of a proper and ennobled democracy.

6.793 With the elite of honor and merit at their core, various institutions—cultural, scientific, educational, sporting, advisory, strategic— should be founded, which are able to exert a moral and intellectual influence on society.

6.8 Sophocracy awakens civic spirit.

6.81 Civic spirit is the active participation of citizens in the process of governance at the local, provincial, and national levels.

6.811 The self-organization of society, expressed in political and cultural initiatives, is a result of civic spirit.

6.812 The basis of civic spirit is the emotional involvement of citizens in the affairs of their own country, resulting in practical involvement in grassroots initiatives.

6.813 Individual or group selfishness, control from above, and vast bureaucracy are contrary to civic spirit.

6.8131 Citizens are themselves able to produce the proper amount of societal power needed for their activities. Bureaucracy is not only unable to create societal power, but usually disturbs and weakens it.

6.814 Civic spirit is a result of the love of liberty, which is the desire to make decisions and govern oneself, and of patriotism, the love of one's country.

6.82 While the highest intellectual and moral qualities can be attained only by a minority—the elite of honor and merit—the majority of citizens, taking the elite as a model, can acquire civic virtues: civil courage, honesty, moderation, respect for the law, diligence, entrepreneurship, and, above all, love of freedom and love of the homeland.

6.821 As Rousseau wrote, giving Poland as an example, the most important factor for the awakening of civic spirit is the "establishment of the Republic in the hearts of Poles."

6.822 Even if cosmopolitan feeling connects us with the whole of humanity, our special love is owed to the nation to which we belong and the place from which we come.

6.823 Our homeland is the country of our fathers—it is our land, to which we are attached by our common language, history, and traditions, as well as by our current common interests and our aspirations for the future.

6.824   The quarrels of our countrymen and any other deficiencies of our home country do not justify us in rejecting it in favor of what we have observed, often very superficially, abroad; on the contrary, such problems necessitate our personal commitment and contribution to our country's repair.

6.825   Love of the homeland requires that we strive for its protection, enhancement, and enrichment.

6.826   Love of the homeland equips citizens with inner strength, enabling them to resist the enslavement and corruption by the modern world.

6.827   Love of one's own country, patriotism, is not associated with hatred of strangers—it is not chauvinism. On the contrary, it teaches us to love all people because it is associated with the love of freedom and wishes all nations the right to self-determination.

6.8271   Love, coming from the depths of the heart, is a virtue and the highest feeling of which human beings are capable.

6.8272   Justice without love easily turns into hatred.

6.8273   If we take away love from human hearts, there will be nothing left in them but selfishness.

6.9   Love is a virtue, a queen among other virtues, complementing them all.

7 The Mystery of Existence

7 We must speak about what we can no longer pass over in silence.
  7.01 Propositions are not of equal value. Some make sense, others are meaningless; some express truth, others are false; some teach us something, others mislead or demoralize us.
    7.1 The sense of the world lies in the world itself. It is determined by culture.
        7.101 Each culture gives people a certain vision of the world.
        7.102 By creating culture, human beings create their own environment, which is the world.
      7.12 In the world created by human beings, nothing is as it is and nothing happens as it does happen. The world undergoes a constant transformation: what is old goes away and what is new arrives.
      7.13 The essence of culture, of the human-made environment, is values.
          7.1301 By creating culture, human beings go beyond their original biological endowment. Values constitute a new driving force for their actions.
      7.14 Every value always has some value.
      7.15 If there are values that have a value, they are a part of everything that happens and takes place in human life.
      7.16 For nothing that happens and is the case is accidental.
          7.1601 The occurrence of human activities depends on the economic, political, moral, and religious values adopted by people.

The entire educational and political system in a given society is determined by the values adopted.

7.17 What makes these activities non-accidental lies, in fact, in the world, because every value, every custom, and every belief is in the world and has a specific social function.

7.18 Values must therefore lie in the world.

7.2 There can be ethical propositions. Speaking with sense about ethics and politics is possible.

7.201 Not only is it possible to apprehend the values that define human traits and actions, and to talk about them with sense; they have actually been a subject of discourse since the beginning of humankind.

7.202 The world is something more than the totality of facts, and propositions can express something higher than facts. That "something higher" is values.

7.2021 The world is the totality of values, rather than the totality of facts.

7.21 Ethics and politics can be expressed and put into practice.

7.2101 Ethics is not transcendental. It is an immanent component of human life, shaped by individual and collective experience and incorporated into a tradition.

7.2102 The subject of ethics is moral values (justice, selflessness, honesty, truthfulness, fidelity) and the subject of aesthetics is aesthetic values (beauty, subtlety, lightness, regularity, proportionality).

7.22 Ethical norms, such as "love your neighbor" or "do no harm," are not something relative, in the sense of a means to a particular end; namely, a means for receiving a reward in the form of satisfaction for performing a good deed or of getting access to "heaven." Love is not a means, but an end. It is the source of ever-resurgent life, on both a material and a spiritual plane. It is through love that human beings and the world are reborn: God's love of human beings, human beings' love of God, and mutual love among people. Love is the essence of excellence—the moral perfection of humanity.

7.23 Our lust or desire can induce the will to a certain action, but whether the action will be taken depends on our rational assessment of the situation and then on our decision. As long we are able to make a choice, we are free. Freedom is the basis of ethics.

7.3 Reality, what-exists, is a multilevel, complex, and dynamic manifold.

7.31 There are three different dimensions of reality: facts, values, and states of consciousness, and others that can still be discovered. Each of them is of relative importance.

7.311 Reality is not merely a set of facts arrested in a process observation. Reality or the world is not determined by facts. All the facts are only one dimension of reality.

7.312 Reality without values lacks one important dimension. Only human beings can think and express values and act according to them.

7.313 States of consciousness refer to knowledge. Without knowledge human beings do not exist; without human beings there is no knowledge.

7.32 Reality is not static. It has its dynamics. It evolves in phases, cosmic, biological, and human, in a process that generates novelty, variety, and sophistication.

7.321 In the current human phase, evolution is no longer related merely to matter, but proceeds through the development of mind.

7.3211 The vehicle of evolution is knowledge.

7.33 The world which gradually emerges and unveils itself to us is real, and should not be regarded as illusion or be associated with sorrow.

7.331 We can experience happiness at different levels. Each of us deserves a flourishing, fulfilling life.

7.3311 Life is not a continual flow of desires, as materialists declare; it is rather a flow of experiences. If those are joyful, good experiences, then our lives become happy.

7.3312 Happiness may be related to joyful life experiences and in a longer perspective to our fulfilment or self-realization, the highest good that human beings usually desire.

7.4 The key to the understanding of reality is human evolution.

    7.41 Without human beings reality would be impoverished.

        7.411 Reality unveils its new layers with the moral and intellectual development of humankind.

    7.42 As humans, we are evolutionary beings, capable of self-transformation and of moral and intellectual improvement.

        7.421 Morality and rationality are dynamic phenomena. They cannot be merely prescribed by unchanging rules, but have to be internalized.

            7.4211 We can still develop greatly our moral sensitivity and learn to apply the rule "do not harm" not only in relation to other human beings, but also to other animals, and even to the natural world at large.

            7.4212 The secret of the world transformation lies in our mind. We change the world, when we change our thinking.

    7.43 Good or bad willing does not change the world, or its limits, but only human choices and actions. Acts of the will lead to good and bad actions. Not just facts, but also values, can be expressed in language.

        7.4301 The world created by human beings is constantly changing.

        7.4302 "The world of the happy is quite another than that of the unhappy" (Ludwig Wittgenstein).

    7.431 The world never comes to an end. The continuity of life is passed along the chain of generations. Only people, nations, cultures, and civilizations perish.

        7.4311 Death can be an event in life. One can observe the deaths of relatives, or of strangers. Death can be lived through. One can live painfully through the death of others and experience a clinical death himself. The fear of death is the fear of what is unknown.

            7.43111 With the flow of time, everything changes. Reality does not have a static quality, but dynamic. It is evolutionary. Therefore, there is no timelessness in the world. Timelessness would be stillness, and stillness is a form of eternity.

7.43112 Human life has an end, and goes by so quickly; therefore, everyone should think how to make it valuable. Life and death are inextricably linked.

7.4312 Reflections on the immortality of the soul fall within the domain of the Absolute Mystery and lie beyond the scope of knowledge accessible by science and philosophy. They can be carried out only on the basis of religion—revealed knowledge.

7.431201 "Where the negative results of strict philosophy end and where begins the Absolute Mystery for all possible minds of individuals who stand at the highest place in the hierarchy of individual [human] beings, there is a place for religion, for people are seriously in need of the general sense of existence whose necessity philosophy is not able to prove" (Stanislaw Ignacy Witkiewicz).

7.431202 "The philosopher aspires to explain away all mysteries, to dissolve them into light. It is the Mystery, on the other hand, which religious instinct demands and to which it aspires" (Henri-Frederic Amiel).

7.432 If "What is Higher" were completely indifferent to how the world was, there would be no religion. By means of the founders of religions and other messengers, God is manifested in this world.

7.43201 Throughout history, selected individuals have interacted with God and from God have received positive energy and their messages.

7.43202 The essence of religion is the unity of the individual "I" with God, of an individual consciousness with the cosmic consciousness—the Supreme Consciousness.

7.43203 The Supreme Consciousness is the source of knowledge and brings about our transformation.

7.43204 Knowledge about the drama here on Earth, and of our high task, gives us a spiritual understanding.

7.43205 The vice that leads humanity to its downfall is pride.

7.43206 The human being is more than the body, and the soul is immortal.

7.43207 The soul wants to return to God.

7.4321 The facts are neither the task nor the solution. The facts simply are. The Mystery of Existence goes beyond knowledge of facts. In order to embrace the Mystery of Existence, we need a spiritual understanding. Because of it we discover our true identity and are directed to our goal, which is moral and intellectual perfection.

7.44 That the world is, is a Mystery of Existence.

7.45 To view the world *sub specie aeternitatis* is to look at it from the perspective of eternity. Looking at it in this way, we suspend our everyday perception of events and feel a metaphysical anxiety.

7.4501 This metaphysical anxiety is a mystical feeling.

7.5 The great riddle exists. By experiencing metaphysical anxiety, we ask about the Mystery of Existence. What is existence? Why does the world exist? How did it come about? Was it created or did it originate by itself? What was there before?

7.51 Metaphysical anxiety is common to all human beings, although it can be suppressed in some. This feeling is expressed in religion and philosophy.

7.52 Even if all possible scientific questions were answered, the problems of philosophy and religion would remain intact. Science is partial knowledge of a part. It apprehends a part of reality with the help of a narrowly specialized conceptual apparatus.

    7.5201 The sum of the parts does not yet form the whole. There would still remain many questions.

    7.521 The question of the meaning of being is the deepest problem of life for every human being. Everyone answers this question alone; and therefore, our answer is not always valid for others.

    7.522 There is indeed something inexpressible in words. This is something that, in revealing itself, touches the Mystery of Existence and transcends the limits of human understanding.

        7.52201 Sometimes what is inexpressible in words can be expressed in feelings.

7.53 Philosophy is a quest for complete knowledge of the whole of reality, not of a mere part. Reality is both what we experience in everyday life and what is unfamiliar, be it the subject of scientific research or an area still unexplored. In this reality, there are people who create culture—their world, which is the world not only of the totality of entities and facts, but above all of values. The starting point for philosophical reflection is always all knowledge accumulated so far, as well as the outside world, considered from the perspective of truth, goodness, and beauty. While there are many directions and schools in philosophy, to protect itself from self-reduction and possible obliteration, philosophy must always refer to the whole.

    7.5301 There is much we can say in addition to the propositions of the natural sciences. Philosophy is neither the activity of elucidating propositions nor a partial knowledge of a part, and cannot be reduced to such.

    7.5302 Philosophy—the love of wisdom, a quest for complete knowledge—presupposes an affective engagement in the world.

7.531 A common feature underlying philosophy and religion is the need for a comprehensive picture of the world, which provides answers to questions that neither science nor ordinary knowledge can fully and satisfactorily answer.

7.53101 Both religion and philosophy ask questions about the whole of existence and the meaning of being, and direct people to life ends that are appropriate to the dignity of human beings. While philosophy arrives at its conclusions by natural means of reason and proof, religion does so through revelation and faith.

7.53102 Philosophy and religion can complement each other, insofar as philosophy does not become atheistic or reductionist, and does not begin to undermine the truths of faith and question the role of religion in society, and religion in turn does not encroach with its dogma into domains that are proper to philosophy and the various sciences, and does not set itself against them.

7.532 The misuse of science occurs when it negates the reasonableness of religious and philosophical issues and when it reduces metaphysical anxiety and other philosophical and religious feelings to fear, hunger, erotic attraction, and other primary biological impulses. This often results in the adoption by the social sciences of the most banal views of life as axioms or assumptions.

7.54 Those who throw away the ladder have no way to return. They are trapped in the world of their own dogma.

7.5401 Philosophical thinking should not throw anything away and should always be prepared to encounter something new and unknown.

7.5402 "If you do not expect what is unexpected, you will never meet it" (Heraclitus).

7.6 Religions are true, insofar as they morally improve human beings.

7.61 Every aspect of culture—architecture, agriculture, industry, commerce, social organizations, health services, the military, the police, law, the sciences, the arts, philosophy, and religion—corresponds to the specific needs of human beings and gives a picture of the general character of their civilization.

7.611 Religion, as a system of beliefs, practices, and rules of conduct, enters into human life wherever human beings find themselves in situations where their own skills and knowledge are eventually powerless. It concerns the ultimate, eternal, and enduring issues of death and human destiny.

7.612 The social meaning of religion lies in the fact that it forms a social bond among people, establishes values related to their conduct, permeates human life by supporting its most important activities, makes people independent of the fleeting trends of their epoch, and gives them spiritual freedom.

7.6121 Religious faith does not need to restrict human autonomy; on the contrary, it can give people a freedom that comes from their confidence in its moral values and their reliance on the supernatural powers in which they believe.

7.6122 Religion is neither "poetry," as Feuerbach wrote, nor the "opium of the people," as proclaimed by Marx, nor a "collective neurosis," as Freud thought.

7.62 Religion is a powerful element of culture and a source of individual and social values. It inspires cooperation, courage, patience, and perseverance. It leads to the integration of the group and reinforces its strength in the face of danger. It provides human beings with spiritual goals and establishes moral rules for their behavior.

7.621 Given the cultural importance of religion, the effort to reduce its impact on society through the latter's laicization, or even to eliminate it in the name of modernization, progress, and the making of a "new man," is a serious misunderstanding.

7.622 The removal of religion from public life leads to an impoverishment of the public sphere.

7.623 The greatest moral and cultural loss of modern humanity is the collapse of traditional beliefs that establish moral values in human beings, and their replacement by religious fundamentalism and secular ideologies.

7.6231 Powerful political and economic pressure groups have an interest in limiting the influence of religion. They oppose religion not for the sake of freedom and a "new humanity," but rather for the sake of their opposites—enslavement and a "new slavery" resulting from uniformity.

7.6232 The interest of all lobbies is the reduction of human beings to the same kind of individual, motivated only by primitive lust. This is because such individuals make ideal consumers, whether for commercial goods or for sex, and are, at the same time (as persons deprived of higher values, such as virtues), easy to manipulate and instigate to quarrel.

7.6233 A response to modernist secularization is the radicalization and politicization of religion in the form of religious fundamentalism, a kind of totalitarianism, which has little in common with traditional religion and constitutes a denial of many of its values.

7.63 The greatest danger for religions is their conflict, often expressed as a civilizational conflict. The struggle between religions or between sects of the same religion is contrary to the very essence of religion, which is spirituality.

7.631 God is one, Truth is one, and one is Perfection, but there are many roads to God, Truth, and Perfection.

    7.6311 Just as there is no single path to the truth in philosophy, so there is no one path to God.

    7.6312 The quest for truth and knowledge about God can be undertaken in many ways. But there is only one timeless spirituality, which may be attained by all people.

    7.6313 Spirituality means moral improvement: non-harming, benevolence, and love, as well as intellectual growth: the acquisition of wisdom and the development of consciousness, allowing in the final instance for direct contact with God.

7.632 In today's situation of large-scale manipulation and escalating conflict in the world, the peace that humanity desperately needs should begin as peace among religions.

    7.6321 Humankind needs peace to develop further and to strive for moral and intellectual perfection.

    7.6322 Peace is today the great task for leaders of all religions.

    7.6323 Peace on Earth produces peace and silence in the soul.

    7.6324 Silence leads us to reflection.

    7.6325 Reflection bestows liberation.

7.7 The time has come for humanity's self-reflection.

    7.71 What is our goal?

    7.72 What do we want to achieve?

    7.73 What will we pass on to future generations?

    7.74 Although this cannot be the subject of a scientific or philosophical proof, we must assume that the human being is more than a body, and the soul is immortal.

    7.75 Each of us should realize our human destiny, which is to perfect ourselves and to complete human evolution.

    7.76 We were not born here on Earth to become consumers or militants.

7.77 Our deepest knowledge is associated with a reminder of who we really are.

7.78 Have faith that you are essentially a soul—a point of light. The original condition of the soul is purity. Only a pure soul, one that is morally purified, can return to God.

    7.781 To be morally pure means doing no harm and being merciful to others, as well as to oneself.

    7.782 Pure souls are jewels of virtue and the embodiment of the joy that comes from human fulfillment.

7.79 Religion cannot persuade us to harm others; and if someone interprets it that way, this is a false interpretation.

7.8 The world that human beings create outside themselves is a result of the values they adopt.

    7.81 It is an illusion that people can build a just society without first being righteous themselves.

    7.82 To have a positive and lasting effect, any revolution must start from the inside; otherwise, it will be another illusion, bringing more harm than good.

7.9 For each change, we need the right person and the right time.

8   Time, War, and Change

8 To understand their world, people need to understand their time.

  8.1 Time is a measure of change. Time, or the spirit of the time, describes the dominant trends of an era.

    8.11 Because the world around us is constantly changing, political leaders should always be prepared to encounter unexpected events and face challenges.

    8.12 Politics, as the art of governing, requires us to continuously predict events that may happen and respond to them in a timely and appropriate manner.

    8.13 Evils can be prevented if they are recognized early enough. "For when the evils that arise have been foreseen (which it is only given to a wise man to see), they can be quickly redressed, but when, through not having been foreseen, they have been permitted to grow in a way that everyone can see them, there is no longer a remedy" (Niccolò Machiavelli).

      8.131 The greatest evil and one of the greatest dangers to humankind is the escalation of hostility and the upsurge of hatred excited by politicians and the media.

        8.1311 Indoctrination in enmity and hatred changes other people into an inhuman object that can be destroyed in battle or used as a means for specific purposes.

        8.1312 The final and most destructive result of collective hatred is war.

  8.2 War is an armed conflict between two or more political units. These units can be blocs of states, states, or non-state actors, such as organized armed resistance groups or terrorist formations.

8.21 War is a distortion of nature. The normal condition of human beings, arising from their nature, is cooperation, not war.

    8.211 Warfare, involving killing, destruction, intimidation, rape, and robbery, is the negation of the idea of peaceful cooperation among people.

8.22 War is not a permanent institution of humanity.

    8.221 War is a threat to everything that has been created by civilization.

    8.222 An inclination to war is a characteristic feature of lower civilizations, in which higher moral values have not developed fully, and which have been dominated by militarism, expansionism, or similar ideologies.

8.23 War is contrary to freedom and the constructive use of culture.

    8.231 War is a tyranny because it compels men to fight against each other and forces those who resist aggression "to imitate and perhaps even to exceed, the brutality of the aggressor" (Michael Walzer).

8.24 War is the most destructive phenomenon and can be justified only in exceptional cases, when it creates values greater than those that it destroys.

    8.241 War should always be the last resort in international politics.

8.25 A war of defense against external aggression is justified because the country that defends itself acts to protect the life and liberty of its citizens and their national culture.

    8.251 To justify the decision to fight, there must be a real chance of winning.

    8.252 A defensive war that, due to a large difference in forces and lack of other means to win, must end in a defeat cannot be justified.

    8.253 The reason for war cannot be honor alone. A single person can die for the sake of honor, but he can never by his act condemn others to death and suffering.

8.2531 A noble person can afford to die in defense of his ideals. Yet, no state can afford to act in this way.

8.254 The moral responsibility for a defensive war waged in the name of honor, and particularly for harm to civilians, falls on both the invaders and the defenders.

8.26 The decision to go to war should always be based on a rational calculation of forces.

8.261 War is an instrument of politics, and not vice versa. In order to be an effective instrument, there must be a reasonable chance of winning.

8.262 Any armed struggle must have clearly defined political objectives and must be based on a real chance of achieving them.

8.263 There are historical cases where a smaller force prevailed over a larger, but these were usually associated with a high level of talent in the command and the superior training and valor of the outnumbered troops.

8.264 Any armed struggle conducted with no chance for success, only for the sake of honor or for the fight itself, and not based on a rational calculation of forces, is a form of collective suicide.

8.27 The justification for war may sometimes be the resultant effects that are enabling for culture, such as the creation of political entities that give people better conditions for development. Based on this principle, there once arose states from tribal organizations, and, conversely, empires or other larger states have been divided into smaller ones.

8.271 War can be constructive for culture, but only when it is limited and carried out according to the rules of war, when violence is the only way to overcome cultural or civilizational barriers, and when in the longer perspective both sides of the conflict receive compensation in the form of a common benefit that causes their cultures to further and better develop.

8.272 According to the stated aims of the second Gulf War (replacing dictatorship with democracy and improving the lives of the local population), we may presume it was meant to be constructive for culture; but the situation in Iraq following the war proves that these expectations have largely failed. This should be a sufficient warning to all who try to play with war and employ it as an easy instrument of policy.

8.2721 Every war is a lesson of history, but that lesson is most often quickly forgotten, deformed, or idealized, and instead of teaching us something, it is molded into an element of ideology and used for purposes of indoctrination.

8.28 The most destructive war is total or ideological war, as it is fought with great ferocity and hatred, and used to mobilize all the resources of a society: human, material, and spiritual.

8.29 A civil war, a fratricidal war, is extremely harmful to both sides engaged in the conflict. It is a wound that is not easy to heal due to the destruction of the common cultural heritage of both sides, which is the basis of their political integration.

8.3 Contemporary wars are potentially much more destructive than the wars known from history. There are material and sociological reasons for this. Never before have human beings developed such means of destruction, and never before have they been equipped with such powerful tools of mass manipulation and indoctrination.

8.31 The destructiveness of war today is also a result of the diminishing influence of traditional morality and religion. Both secularized antireligiosity and religious fundamentalism reject any moral limitations on action.

8.311 "When no restrictions, no moral forces, and no rational influences relate human beings to certain ideals, they can become cruel and predatory beasts" (Bronislaw Malinowski).

8.4 Wars are subject to limitation on the basis of their cause and conduct.

8.41 The limitation of wars is not only possible but, because of natural law and existing international conventions, also fully justified.

    8.411 Since the basic principle of natural law is not harming others, the only just causes of war are self-defense and aiding those who are attacked. The greater the objections with reference to the justice of a war's cause, the more its conduct should meet the requirements of morality.

8.42 War should always, regardless of the behavior of the other side, be conducted according to the rules of war. Those who do not apply these rules debase their civilization.

    8.421 The rules of war are the principles of justice and honor applied to warfare.

    8.422 Moderation on one side of a conflict produces moderation on the other, and the lack of moderation on one side results in a lack of moderation on both.

    8.423 The purpose of any armed struggle is to win and to protect one's own side against death, and in such circumstances, it is sometimes very difficult to apply moral principles. However, due to their ability to win wars in accordance with the accepted rules of war and their gentle handling of prisoners and the peoples of conquered lands, nations can gain the reputation of being righteous. This opinion allows them to consolidate their rule over others.

8.43 According to the theory of just war, which has a long tradition and has been referred to in many international conventions, those who do not participate in fighting should not be killed deliberately. These comprise civilians and soldiers who surrender or are wounded.

    8.431 All sides of a conflict must do everything possible to protect civilians from harm.

    8.432 The use of terror against a civilian population by deliberately bombing populated areas, destroying homes, attacking civilians, carrying out mass executions, and setting up death camps is an indication of cruelty and is not approved by any religion. Such acts violate the rules of war and the ethical standards that are obligatory for all humankind.

8.44 Terror may not be justified on the basis of its use as a method of inspiring fear in the other side.

8.441 No state that keeps subjugated people in check through force and fear, and poisons them with hatred, can long withstand the hatred of the many.

8.442 Those who put themselves in positions of inspiring fear in others must in fact be afraid of those whom they want to intimidate.

8.443 Fear reinforces fear; hate breeds hatred; violence leads to more violence. This rule applies to situations in both domestic and international politics.

8.4431 No one has ever won any war by means of fear alone.

8.4432 People hate those whom they fear.

8.4433 Mass fear causes mass dehumanization and increases hatred, and with the escalation of hatred the possibility of a peaceful solution to a conflict is diminished.

8.4434 When there is no longer any chance for peace, there remains only a struggle for life and death, similar to that which took away 60 million lives during World War II.

8.44341 We should consider why they died. What have we actually achieved together because of this war?

8.444 History teaches us that in politics, people make mistakes, and that all powers inspiring fear will fall.

8.445 Fear is an unreliable defense—unlike human goodwill, which remains in the memory forever, connects people, and builds civilization.

8.45 For any society, contamination by hostility and hatred toward others, militarization, and a constant readiness for war are demoralizing and destructive.

8.451 The achievements of culture cannot resist the destructive influence of war. War is the opposite of everything that a highly developed culture values.

8.452 War creates a common atmosphere on both sides of a conflict. It produces destructive predispositions. It converts the entire energy of society to a desire to destroy the enemy.

8.453 If power becomes the highest value of life, brutality pays off, and ruthlessness and violence become the basis of a state policy, then its civilization is endangered.

8.46 In contrast to earlier wars that were waged according to the rules of honor by the knighthood or professional armies trained in the art of war, today's wars are not a test of courage and do not improve individual or group skills. They have become almost without exception a mechanical murder of innocent people—murder in which terror and pressure groups, arms manufacturers, and financial organizations are implicated.

8.5 Wars are often delusions of those who count on an easy victory.

8.51 How shortsighted and how mistaken are those who believe in power alone!

8.511 Power is a fragile basis of security, and policy based on power alone is, in the end, ineffective. This was noticed even by Machiavelli, who wrote that "a single act of tenderness, mercy, chastity, or generosity" could sometimes do more than "the instruments and engines of war."

8.512 The real power of a society, greater than its military power, is its moral power. This should be well taken care of. Thanks to this power, a nation can persist and survive.

8.6 Some conflicts and wars can be considered intra-epochal, and others inter-epochal.

8.61 For the traditional societies of the past, conflicts and wars were intra-epochal. Wars were caused mainly by economic, ethnic, dynastic, religious, and civilizational conflicts.

8.62   In the age of modernity, the most characteristic wars took place between nation-states or blocs of states and were conducted on economic or ideological grounds; there were many wars of national liberation as well.

8.63   Modern wars are both intra-epochal and inter-epochal conflicts.

    8.631   The inter-epochal conflict is a clash of epochs.

8.7   The clash of epochs is a conflict between traditionalism, modernity, and postmodernity.

    8.71   The clash of epochs, which begins in times of modernity, has led to a profound transformation of human life: from the traditional, based on traditional cultural unity, through the modern, whose expression is the sovereign nation-state, to the postmodern, whose expression is globalization.

        8.711   Samuel Huntington argued that the conflict between civilizations would be the last phase in the evolution of conflict in the modern world. My thesis is that the clash of epochs is far more fundamental.

        8.712   The most fundamental conflict of the modern world is the clash of epochs.

            8.7121   The clash of epochs is the hitherto insufficiently noticed ground on which different forms of conflicts, including the current conflict between civilizations, take place.

    8.72   Traditionalism (or the age of traditional society), modernity, and postmodernity are three epochs (historical periods) and at the same time three ideological and cultural formations.

        8.721   Ideological or cultural formations are characterized by the "simultaneity of what is not simultaneous" (Ernst Bloch). They can exist side by side in different historical periods.

            8.7211   In modern times, we can find still traditional societies and many people who still think in a traditional way.

        8.722   The key concepts, and also values, that can be associated with a traditional society are family, morality, religiosity, and community. These are values that are common to many civilizations, including the traditional Western European civilization.

8.723 The organizing principle of a traditional society is the common culture, which consists of manners and customs, religious values, and traditional morality. These are the bonds linking the community together.

8.73 Modernity (or the modern era) is the epoch in which the countries of the West achieved an unprecedented dominance over the rest of the world due to the development of science and technology.

8.731 Modernity is not only a historical period, but also a certain ideological or cultural formation.

8.7311 As an ideological formation, modernity signifies a set of ideas and attitudes toward the world.

8.7312 The key concepts, and also values, associated with modernity include freedom, rationality, and belief in progress, as well as national unity and state sovereignty.

8.73121 Modern rationality is an imperfect form of rationality because it narrows its scope of inquiry. It is based on the conviction that all human problems can eventually be solved by science, and what cannot be rationally justified (custom, religion) should be rejected.

8.732 The modern state, which is a sovereign nation-state, claims a monopoly on the legitimate use of physical force. It bases its legitimacy on the sovereignty of the people—that is, the sovereignty of free and equal individuals—and on this ground challenges the traditional, hierarchical social system. It shapes the identity of its citizens in accordance with the principle of rationalism and a belief in progress.

8.7321 In the process of forming the modern state, traditional communities, identities, and loyalties are replaced by a modernist society organized according to the principles of reason. Traditional morality and religiosity are weakened. Consequently, there occurs an erosion of traditional society.

8.733 Modernity overturns the ideas and values of the traditional (classical and Christian) culture of the West, and, once it becomes global, leads to the erosion of non-European traditional cultures. Further destruction of traditional thinking and ways of life is brought about by postmodernity, which represents a challenge to modernity but is at the same time a radical continuation of the modern project.

8.74 In his book *The End of History and the Last Man*, Francis Fukuyama predicts the triumph of liberal democracy over other forms of government, and the end of history. The end of history signifies, according to him, "the end point of mankind's ideological evolution and the universalization of Western liberal democracy as the final form of human government." He believes that humankind has, in liberal democracy, discovered a perfect form of government, and therefore ideological struggles should end, and there should no longer be any need for political philosophy.

8.741 Liberal democracy is a modern creation. Its triumph signifies the final establishment and victory of modernity. Has modernity indeed been finally victorious? Is our contemporary era identical to modernity, and should we not expect anything more in the future?

8.742 Modernity is today being challenged by postmodernity, which is a very recent phenomenon. The way for its coming was prepared by technology, economics, and politics, but above all by this undervalued philosophy.

8.75 The key concepts that can be associated with postmodernity are difference, diversity, multiculturalism, deconstruction, and globalization.

8.751 The beginnings of postmodernity can be associated with the end of the Cold War and the collapse of communism in Europe, because these events on the one hand removed the restrictions on world trade and opened the gates for globalization, while on the other they led to the rise of a new, post-Marxist and postmodernist critical thought.

8.752 The postmodernists criticize modern rationality and rationalization as tools of planning and control, and deny that there is any privileged— objective, rational, and particularly European or Western—way of looking at reality. They thereby undermine the superior role of the West in the development of a universal culture of humankind.

8.753 Whereas modernity privileges reason and the modernist Western culture that stands behind it, in postmodernity both are dethroned. In postmodern thought, both rationality and Eurocentric perspectives, which are associated with dominance, are removed and replaced with multiculturalism and the celebration of difference.

8.754 The intellectual avant-garde of postmodernity criticizes modern rationality and, at the same time, denigrates the values of traditional society.

8.76 Both modernity and postmodernity are a threat to traditional communities and to traditional morality and religiosity.

8.761 Traditionalism has its source in an organic picture of the world; modernity, drawing heavily from Byzantism, in a mechanical view. The former sees natural differences among human beings, while the latter assumes their social homogeneity.

8.7611 In the name of the truths of reason and empirically verifiable knowledge, modernity refutes truths based on faith and custom. Modern individualism contributes to the destruction of traditional social ties and replaces them with groupings of people with similar interests or an artificially constructed national unity.

8.762 Postmodernity, in turn, undermines the national unity of the modern state through its notions of diversity and multiculturalism. It weakens the nation-state and deconstructs its sovereignty. By its affirmation of diversity in relation to sexual preferences, it also weakens the traditional family based on heterosexual relationships.

8.77 Due to the influence of the ideology of postmodernity, traditional and modernist Western civilization is undergoing a process of deconstruction.

8.771 Postmodernity has been rightly described as a "post-Western phenomenon."

8.7711 Postmodernity weakens the West. It provides a historical opportunity for the Orient, the shadowy "Other" of the Occident, to come into dominance.

8.772 "Postmodernity dethrones modernity and decenters Eurocentrism" (Hwa Yol Jung).

8.7721 Postmodernity decentralizes the West internally by removing its cultural heritage from a central, privileged position in Western societies, and externally by allowing its Asian competitors to grow in power, thus gradually moving it from the economic center to the periphery.

8.7722 The internal deconstruction of Western societies can be related to the postmodern idea of multiculturalism. The modern politics of national identity on the basis of cultural unity is replaced by the promotion of cultural diversity.

8.773 Multiculturalism is articulated not only in the fact of the existence in one country of many ethnic groups and cultures, but also in a normative commitment to the recognition of the plurality of coexisting cultures, without highlighting any of these cultures as the dominant one, as a positive value. It places value on heterogeneity and diversity rather than homogeneity and unity.

8.7731 The danger inherent in the promotion of multiculturalism is that it dethrones the dominant national culture and leads to the splitting of society into separate cultural groups, each claiming its distinctiveness.

8.7732 The breakdown of society into separate cultural groups removes the stable foundation of society, which is based on cultural unity, and is especially dangerous when, along with cultural diversity, there also exists a civilizational conflict. It contributes to a potentially unstable environment, in which culture wars can be inflamed.

8.77321 Conflict between civilizations within a society can be operative at this level.

8.77322 The policy of bringing cultures that come from different civilizations into close contact and denying that one of them—the native national culture—has a dominant role in society causes a sense of insecurity among citizens who identify with the native culture. This gives rise to anti-immigrant movements and ethnic clashes, as we may frequently witness in Europe and other parts of the world.

8.7733 The positive value of multiculturalism is questionable if it leads society to division and conflict.

8.78 To avoid civilizational conflict, the culture of a society should be based on the dominant native culture, while ensuring tolerance for others.

8.781 Nativeculturalism—the principle of domination in society of the native national culture, with tolerance for other cultures—is of particular importance for older countries; those that have for centuries developed on the basis of one dominant culture.

8.782 Parentsexuality is similarly an answer to today's multisexuality, which leads to the collapse of the family and the destruction of the entire society.

8.7821 Parentsexuality is the principle of privileging in society the traditional sexual relationship between a man and a woman, who unite to establish a family and to have children.

8.7822 Parentsexuality, privileging a traditional sexuality, is a response to multisexuality, namely, the postmodern idea that there is no longer any privileged sexual orientation, just a diversity of desires.

8.7823 Without traditional parental sexuality, society is doomed to extinction, and should it not die first on its own, it will be dominated or conquered by sexually traditional societies based on large families.

8.783 The ideas of postmodernity that internally weaken the West today are unlikely to have a similar impact on the East.

8.7831 The postmodern idea of multiculturalism helps Islamic fundamentalists to win themselves a place in Western societies, but their goal is not tolerance or pluralism; it is to organize social life according to their religious principles.

8.7832 Because of their religion and traditions, it is inconceivable that Muslim countries will develop into postmodern societies that will embrace multiculturalism.

8.7833 The residents of the Far East are practical people, interested in developing skills, obtaining tangible effects, and consolidating power, rather than in promoting diversity and conducting fruitless intellectual speculation.

8.7834 Confucian practicality fits perfectly into the Lockean model of the "industrious and rational" individuals who built modern Western capitalism; consequently, it makes the Far Eastern countries tough competitors in world markets.

8.79 Our time is the age of postmodernity and of the clash of epochs. But a new age of humanity is rising. It is *evolutionity* or the evolutionary epoch which replaces modernity and postmodernity.

8.791 In postmodernity, which is rooted in the project of modernity and constitutes its extension, there lies a contradiction. It causes an erosion of the principles of efficiency and rationality, which are the basis of modernity and of the competitiveness of societies vis-à-vis each other in general.

8.7911 Postmodernity can be regarded as merely a short-lived episode in the history of humankind, but one nonetheless fraught with consequences. Postmodernity, which coincides with globalization and weakens the state, has led to political irrationalism, resulting in the disappearance of professional diplomacy.

8.79111 The effects of postmodernity are continued political instability and uncontrolled violence.

8.79112 Instead of benefiting from technological progress and living in an increasingly better world, we live in a world that is becoming more dangerous and less predictable.

8.792 Postmodernity, whose practical expression is globalization, does not lead humanity to a better, more peaceful world.

8.793 While modernity was inspired by the mechanistic, materialistic, and deterministic view of the universe and tried to apply this view to social phenomena, and postmodernity has been characterized by unsolved problems related to globalization and a regress to irrationality, the evolutionary epoch or evolutionity is inspired by the organic and holistic worldview emerging from new scientific theories and the idea of human evolution.

8.7931 Evolutionity is not a revolutionary epoch, but evolutionary. It is not against traditions, but rather tries to build on their values. It does not want to undermine religions, but seeks to uncover what is truly valuable in them—their spirituality.

8.7932 As we are now entering into the age of evolutionity, we become increasingly aware about our identity and our task, which is to further develop morally and intellectually and to complete human evolution. Through our striving for perfection, the world will be transformed.

8.8 America is not merely a continent or a country. It is a symbol of the world's transformation.

8.81 Locke once declared that "in the beginning all the world was America." We may follow in this line of thought by saying that, in the end, all the world will be America again.

8.811 The beginning to which Locke refers is a world without money and commerce, a state of nature, which he, perhaps wrongly, identifies with the American continent of his time, before it was colonized. The end, as things stand at present, appears to be the triumph of global commerce and finance.

8.812 Although the transformation process does not always proceed smoothly, and occasional resistance is encountered, the whole world follows America and is being transformed according to one model.

8.8121 This model is not derived from classical-Christian culture. It is based on the notion of self-interested, pleasure-seeking, and power-hungry individuals whose conception we have inherited from modernity: individuals who are restrained neither by religion, nor by natural law, nor by the mores of traditional society.

8.82 The end of the Cold War and the momentary triumph of liberal democracy accelerated the process of globalization, which has led to the opening of new opportunities and has stimulated human expectations and desires to a degree unknown before.

  8.821 Globalization has unleashed an unbounded commercial zeal, impelling people to ignore all boundaries and look for profit in even the most remote corners of the world.

  8.8211 At the same time, globalization has further eroded traditional societies and contributed to the decline of traditional morality and the loss of a sense of what is right and proper.

  8.8212 While providing new opportunities for acquiring wealth and bringing distant cultures into closer contact, globalization has also produced environmental damage, economic asymmetries, and social tensions.

  8.8213 Caught in a huge web of global political and economic ties, the state has been weakened. Many states have consequently turned into weak and failed states.

  8.822 The process of globalization cannot be stopped. It is inevitable that we will live in an increasingly interconnected world. What can be avoided is the presentation of globalization and the ideas of postmodernity as positive normative values.

  8.823 Globalization along with postmodernity represent the final breakdown of cultural constraints and the triumph of desires.

  8.8231 Equipped with the newest technological achievements and the vastest powers, humanity is returning to a state of primitivism.

  8.8232 Is there a way out? A reversal occurs at deep night, when spirituality is in decline and when love seems to be almost completely overcome by strife (Empedocles).

It involves the world transformation, a radical reorganization of our dominant system of ideas and beliefs.

8.83 Leadership truly belongs to one who can lead.

8.831 To provide future leadership, America needs to revitalize the tradition of the founders, who like many subsequent generations of Americans, believed that democracy and virtue can be harmoniously brought together.

8.832 At the same time, America, which is now moving beyond the period of its youth, needs to look deeper into its Self and discover spirit beyond the commercial one.

8.9 To solve contemporary problems creatively, and to go beyond postmodernity, humanity needs to return to the tradition of classical rationality.

9 Power and Political Rationalism

9 Power is the ability to act.
  9.1 Power is the ability to both give and receive, build and destroy, do good and do harm.
    9.11 As the ability to do something, power has no value in itself; its value is necessarily related to the goal of an action, which is some particular good.
    9.12 Power is a prerequisite for a good state. The power of a state is the result of the strength of its economy, its capacity to defend itself, and the civic virtues of its citizens.
    9.13 The purpose of politics is a good life, the prosperity or well-being of citizens, and power is an instrument for attaining this.
      9.131 Prosperity or well-being (material and spiritual) is the purpose and most important concept of politics.
      9.132 Power does not define politics, because it is only its instrument.
      9.133 Power must always refer to some good.
  9.2 The power of reason is the ability to think.
    9.21 The ability to think, that is, rationality, is an ability to create concepts and combine them together in a conscious, logical, consistent, and purposive way.
      9.211 Instrumental rationality—which is characteristic of thinking of modernity—takes reasoning to be calculation—thinking about the optimal use of available resources to achieve the desired goals.
      9.212 In classical or deliberative rationality, reasoning is not only an instrument to achieve various benefits, but primarily an axiological reflection on

what is morally good or bad, favorable or unfavorable, right or wrong.

9.213 The opposite of rationality in politics is political inanity, the second most serious disease of democracy after usurpation.

9.2131 Political *inanity* involves acting on the emotions of others by means of inducing controversies.

9.21311 Controversies are empirically unverifiable issues that divide public opinion.

9.21312 Political inanity is a result of the deficiency of logical thinking, and, in particular, the result of erroneous (not based on valid proof) interpretation and incorrect association of facts (connecting them without logical and empirically proven relationships), and of making hasty generalizations.

9.214 Classical rationality is reasoning based on logic and empirical evidence. Its range covers the whole of human culture.

9.215 Classical rationality, which is grounded in a conviction of the rational nature of human beings and of human dignity as a consequence of this rational nature, has given birth to philosophy and to science.

9.216 Classical rationality is expressed in politics in the pragmatism of actions aimed at a good life.

9.3 Politics should always be rational.

9.31 Rational politics is pragmatic and free of ideology.

9.32 The right approach to politics is political rationalism.

9.321 Political rationalism assumes that human beings are endowed with reason and that as a result of their rationality they are able to acquire knowledge and create culture; in particular, they are able to conceptually grasp reality and formulate and verify theories.

9.33 Is political thinking that is not ideological possible? Yes, this is open thinking—not dogmatic, but pragmatic.

9.34 Knowledge is threefold: pragmatic—if its object is efficient action; theoretical—if its object is learning; and ideological—if its object is controlling and subduing others.

9.341 The purpose of pragmatic knowledge is the good; of theoretical knowledge, the truth; of ideological knowledge, a dogma.

9.3411 Pragmatic knowledge is expressed in practical disciplines: politics, ethics, economics, medicine, military strategy, and others.

9.3412 In politics, the purpose, or the good, is prosperity or a good life; in ethics, virtue; in economics, material wealth; in medicine, health; and in military strategy, victory.

9.342 Ideological knowledge is ideology or doctrinairism. It is always based on dogmas—that is, on claims that one cannot verify by subjecting them to critical examination, but must be accepted without question and often under coercion.

9.3421 Like pragmatic knowledge, ideological knowledge is action-oriented; however, while in pragmatic knowledge the emphasis is on the effectiveness of actions intended to benefit all people, ideological knowledge is used to control human behavior through specific assertions that are dogmas.

9.3422 Secular dogmas are distinct from religious ones. While the latter are the results of revealed truth, which can be neither confirmed nor refuted rationally, secular dogmas (for example, the inevitability of class struggle) are the result of human invention and can be refuted. If they cannot be disproved on theoretical grounds, then they can at least be shown as false on the basis of practice, because as elements of ideology implemented in social life, secular dogmas do not stand the test of time and of collective human experience.

9.3423 There is something astounding in the fact that despite the existence of widespread public education and highly advanced science and technology, ideologies still come back to assume new forms, such that in politics it is difficult to replace them with thinking of a pragmatic nature.

9.34231 The only explanation for the continuous return of ideologies is their inventors, the ideologues themselves.

9.34232 Ideologues are so attached to their dogmas that they discover they were wrong only when their entire world is already collapsing. But even then they do not return to the world of goodness and truth, but quickly find another ideology for themselves.

9.343 Wise people learn from sages or wise books, ordinary people from ideologues and from the consequences of the crises and wars they live through.

9.3431 The sage is a wise and dignified person.

9.3432 To recognize a sage, we need to become wise ourselves.

9.3433 We need to find among ourselves wise and noble persons, individuals with a sense of tradition.

9.3434 Someone whose grandfather was a communist and whose father was a Stalinist, and who was himself previously a liberal before becoming a conservative, does not look like a person coming from a family of tradition, but rather from one that always makes revolution and attempts to maintain itself in power.

9.35 Rationalism in politics expresses itself in the pragmatism of action, aiming at a good life; and in the knowledge of the highest goals of humanity and of everyday human behavior.

9.36 Our world is real, and pragmatic knowledge has real consequences. These consequences are material, social, and spiritual.

9.37 To come to the suitable result, a good life in society, we need both the right people, i.e., those who are wise, and the proper knowledge, that which is pragmatic, serves to promote human cooperation, and is devoid of any dogma.

9.38 If we reflect on the course of history, we shall understand how many states owe their unparalleled growth to the decisions of leaders (an example would be Kemal Atatürk) who did not hesitate to go beyond previously established patterns and lay before their countries new, bold strategic directions.

9.381 Atatürk's saying, "Peace at home, peace abroad," should always be a guiding principle for all statesmen.

9.4 A rational approach to foreign policy is rationalism in international relations.

9.41 Rationalism in international relations is a complex theory that vanquishes the extremes of political realism, idealism, critical theory, and postmodernism.

9.411 Rationalism must not be identified with neorealism and neoliberalism, which are attempts to make the theory of international relations more scientific and to take as their model the exact sciences. Their approach can be described as scientism.

9.4111 Scientism is a flawed approach to international relations because it omits in its analyses the most important domain of human culture, the domain of values.

9.4112 Reflections on values cannot be made scientific on the model of physics, or geometry; therefore, one cannot make politics into an exact science. Politics is an art.

9.4113 Politics can be regarded as a humanist discipline, one that embraces values and the complexity of human life. It not only describes what we are doing, but also articulates what we ought to be doing.

9.42 Political realism emphasizes the importance of power in international relations and tries to solve conflicts among states by balancing the power of some with a proportionate power of others, and by looking for limited cooperation among states based on their common interests.

9.421 The main drawback of political realism is its dogmatic character. It is based on stereotypes, such as a universal desire for power, the inevitable egoism of states, the character of politics as a struggle for power, the presence of war as a permanent institution of humanity, and the lack of progress in international relations.

9.4211 The so-called realists maintain that they begin their investigations "with human nature as it actually is, and with the historical processes as they actually take place" (Hans Morgenthau), but in fact they base their theories on a picture of reality that they themselves construct—a picture that is stereotypical or even false.

9.4212 Realism, especially in its extreme form, *Realpolitik*, often expresses skeptical or even cynical opinions regarding the possibility of applying ethics to politics.

9.422 Since they either are not aware or do not accept the idea of human evolution, the "realists" believe there is never-ending conflict between states, and there is no room for progress in international relations. Therefore, the problem of states' security can be solved either by strengthening one's own state (and removing or weakening competitors as they arise), so that no other state can ever imperil it, or by a radical change of the international system—altogether eliminating independent states and replacing them with a world state.

9.4221 Both of these solutions are wrong. First, no power lasts forever. There has never been and never will be any state that can continually dominate all others and, thereby, the whole world. In addition, the removal or weakening of other states that are considered as hostile or belonging to an "axis of evil" increases conflicts and leads to wars, and thus contradicts the idea of security itself. Second, a world state, if it were to come about at all and could actually survive, would be a triumph of centralism and bureaucracy, and would lead humankind to a standstill. If it lacked virtues, it would be a vast operating field for corruption. Moreover, it is doubtful that the world state would improve the security situation of humanity. Violent conflicts would still continue within it, but instead of states, the participants in conflicts would be non-state actors.

9.423 Rationalism is true political realism; not a realism based on simplifications and stereotypes, but one that takes into account the whole of reality, with both its virtues and its flaws, its ups and its downs, its possibilities and its perils.

9.4231 Political rationalism shows humanity a way out from the world of today to a world of greater perfection. It is an evolutionary theory of international relations.

9.43 Idealism provided a theoretical basis for the creation of the League of Nations and later the United Nations. Along with the similar liberal approach, it is the basis for the theory of common security, cooperation, and integration in international relations.

9.431 The main drawbacks of classical idealism are naivety and moralism. Idealists do not place sufficient emphasis on the role of power in international relations, and while overestimating the possibility of cooperation among states, they do not pay enough attention to the differences among them and to pertinent, real threats.

9.4311 Idealists naively believe that international law or signed agreements can stop states from action when it comes to their vital interests; that the friendship and selfless assistance to be found among students at school also appear in relations among states; and that a change in states' form of government to democracy will effectively remove civilizational differences between states, reconcile their interests, and bring about lasting peace. Instead of focusing on states' real interests and seeking real opportunities to resolve conflicts among them by eliminating their differences and identifying common interests, idealists employ moralism or a moral rhetoric, which often is two-faced.

9.4312 The duplicity of moralism consists in a double standard. States that are perceived as hostile are criticized, and their leaders insulted, while states that are perceived as allies are not criticized, and often even supported, despite engaging in similar acts (aggression, crimes against the civilian population).

9.44 The critical theory developed from Marxism is aimed at the emancipation of humanity from all forms of exploitation and emphasizes the community of all people on Earth, which is world society.

9.441 A weakness of critical theorists is that in their quest for universal emancipation they do not see a positive value in the nation and the state. The nation is a cultural entity, contributing positively to the development of civilization, and the state is a political entity that is associated with

discrimination and exploitation only in the case
of defective political regimes.

9.442 Paradoxically, the value of the state has increased
considerably in the era of globalization, when it
is penetrated by multinational corporations and
thereby clearly weakened. The good state serves
liberty. It is the main protector of society against
exploitation and enslavement by foreign capital
and pressure groups.

9.45 Postmodern theory emphasizes the value of diversity.

9.451 The disadvantage of postmodernism is that it is
unable to see diversity in a multitude of nations
and social classes, and in mutually complementary values, and thus reduces diversity to relativ-
ism and nihilism.

9.452 Postmodernists also have a tendency to reduce
the whole of knowledge to an ideology that lacks
any objectivity. They boil down the knowledge
of society to "narratives" that serve the interests
of specific groups.

9.5 Rationalism in international relations, an evolutionary theory
of international relations, is based on seven principles.

9.51 The main objective of international politics is to build a
strong international community based on shared values,
respect for international law, and cooperation in advancing
the prosperity, progress, and perfection of all humanity.

9.52 It is natural for human beings to create culture and build
a world based on values. International relations should
uphold values that are right for life, and in particular
the highest values, on which depend the full moral and
intellectual development of human beings and their
happiness.

9.53 Human beings can fully develop and achieve happiness in conditions of freedom and the diversity ensuing
from freedom. The multiplicity of countries and cultures
should be preserved. An imposed uniformity is contra-
dictory to humanity's yearning for development.

9.54 People and states are guided in their actions by their
own interests, which they perceive as beneficial for

themselves. Even very dissimilar interests can be reconciled with each other. The security of a state is the
result of a proper recognition and understanding of the
interests of other states, skillful conflict resolution, and a
pragmatic calculation of the forces and means of action
leading to the desired goals. The expression of an effective policy is the peaceful resolution of international conflicts. War should always be the last resort.

9.55 Politics, as an art of governing, is not autonomous with
reference to other subject areas, such as economics or
law, but rather superior to them because it arranges the
whole of social life. Since it organizes society for cooperation on the basis of specific values, it is inseparable
from ethics. The basic concept of politics is a good life or
prosperity and not power or interest defined in terms of
power. The power of the state determines its ability to act
and serve its objectives, such as the security, wealth, and
liberty of its citizens, its own independence, and cooperation with other countries.

9.56 The role of any social theory is not only describing and
explaining the world, but also, since the world is far
from perfect, making proposals for its improvement.
Political rationalism makes such a proposal. It aims
at increasing cooperation among people and at eliminating exploitation, poverty, discrimination, terror,
and enmity. It opposes organizations and institutions
that instead of seeing people as an end in themselves,
attempt to use them as a means to an end. In the range
of its proposals for improvement, it includes both
international society and world society.

9.57 Rationalism is aware of the civilizational and cultural
differences that divide humankind, as well as of human
flaws, such as greed, laziness, hatred, jealousy, and selfishness. It battles these vices with human virtues—patience,
maturity, gentleness, wisdom, love, courage, diligence,
entrepreneurship, honesty, and determination—and the
power of tolerance and cooperation. It grounds cooperation among peoples in the world on the values that can

unite them rather than divide them. It works for the sake of peace and prosperity for all.

9.6 Foreign policy must be based on professional diplomacy.

  9.61 The art of diplomacy consists in effectively looking for common interests and values in situations of difference.

    9.611 The contradiction of diplomacy is the rhetoric of hostility.

    9.612 To resolve an international conflict, one should never arouse enmity and escalate hatred. One should rather, despite the differences dividing the sides of the conflict, build between them a relationship based on mutual respect and the reconciliation of differing interests.

  9.62 Diplomacy is a way to obtain benefits for the state by peaceful means.

    9.621 Professional diplomacy always defines precisely the benefits to be obtained.

    9.622 The benefits to be obtained by diplomacy derive from the fundamental interest of each country, which is its national interest.

      9.6221 The national interest must be realistic and precisely defined.

      9.6222 The principal interest of each state is the protection of its political independence, its cultural heritage, and its material wealth.

    9.623 The benefits to be obtained by diplomacy must always be based on the actual or attainable power of the state.

    9.624 An attempt to obtain benefits without sufficient power is the sign of a lack of rationality in politics and can be described as political inanity in the context of international relations.

    9.625 While determining the benefits to be obtained for its own country, diplomacy also defines benefits that can be proposed as advantageous to the state with which talks are being conducted.

  9.63 Moralism—accusations directed against the other side, based on supposed moral grounds—is contrary to diplomatic professionalism.

9.631 Behind moralism is hidden political inanity or interests of the side that employs it.

9.64 Arousing enmity and escalating hatred in the media cannot replace diplomacy.

9.65 Diplomacy should precede war and seek to prevent it.

9.66 War is always a last resort when states' interests cannot be in any way reconciled.

9.67 When war precedes diplomacy, this implies a lack of good will on one of the sides in regard to conducting talks.

9.7 A characteristic of the righteous person is an aversion to quarrels and wars.

9.71 Disputes between human beings can be settled either by discussion or by violence. Violence is characteristic of wild beasts, whereas a defining characteristic of humans is the ability to talk and negotiate.

9.711 In certain circumstances, war to save a state cannot be avoided. Still, one should always avoid wanton cruelty and the infliction of suffering in situations that are not directly related to combat.

9.72 The relevant body of arbitration to resolve international conflicts today is the United Nations, which implements a system of collective security. Despite the shortcomings of this organization, there is no better alternative to it.

9.721 The effectiveness of the system of collective security depends on the strength of the powers comprising it and the values they represent. It can be effective if the major world powers are interested in strengthening international society, rather than in achieving their own individual gains at the expense of other countries.

9.722 Solitary states that rely solely on their own strength and are engaged in an ongoing struggle with each other for survival and domination over others cannot be an alternative to the international society built by the United Nations and its system of collective security.

9.7221 The picture of international relations as an endless violent conflict, which is offered to us by Hans Morgenthau, Kenneth Waltz, and other political "realists," does not solve the problem of war and does not provide any vision for the progress of and a better future for humanity.

9.73 An alternative to an international society linked by ties of cooperation and common values is likewise not a world state, which would deprive individual states of their independence.

    9.731 A world state whose model, as envisioned by the Eurocrats, is the European Union would, like the European Union, represent a triumph of centralism and bureaucracy, and would quickly lead humanity to a standstill, provided it were not in the meantime ripped apart by a grim civilizational conflict.

9.8 In a situation where there exists a diversity of many states, the stability of the international system is ensured by a hegemon, if it is decent.

    9.81 A hegemon is a strong state whose power allows it to rise above all other states and perform the role of a leader among them.

    9.82 Hegemony is not a form of world government, but rather the informal (based on authority and influence, not law) leadership of other states by a hegemonic state.

        9.821 The exercise of hegemony can be regarded as the actions taken by a single predominant state in pursuit of its own national self-interest, which also provide benefits, such as security, cultural exchange, and economic development, for other states.

        9.822 Respect of the norms of cooperation within the framework of international society may seem inconsistent with the interests of a strong state, which, if it wants, can maintain or even enlarge its power and territory at the expense of other states. However, such a policy in the end gives that state long-term benefits resulting from international cooperation and the enhancement of its own security.

9.83 To lead others in an upright and just manner, one must serve them. A decent hegemon performs its leadership function through acts of service and justice toward others, not through oppression.

    9.831 The leadership of a decent hegemon consists of care for the world, rather than its domination. The hegemon attains its own national interest, but its role in the world also brings benefits to countries that are cooperating with it.

    9.832 To be a decent hegemon and not invite opposition, the predominant state cannot rely solely on its "hard power," i.e., its ability to get others to do what it wants because of its superior military and economic capacities; it also needs "soft power," that is, moral authority. It must influence others by its ideas and values.

    9.833 Despite its size and strength, a decent hegemon allows its actions to be evaluated by its allies and carries out its policies in a way that does not alienate them. By upholding the principles of peace and justice in the international forum and by serving other nations, it gains their loyalty and support.

9.84 When a hegemon begins to disregard the principles of peace and justice, and ceases to listen to the voice of world public opinion, it turns into a despot, whose power intimidates others, and that owes its position in the international arena to its military power alone.

    9.841 Instead of promoting international cooperation and protecting the principles of justice in the mutual relations of states, the despotic superpower, a former decent hegemon, begins to manifest its power and violates good neighborly customs and international law. It may even resort to deception and the manipulation of public opinion.

    9.842 The despotic superpower causes worry among its neighbors and thus creates its own opponents.

It changes its former friends into rivals, and its former rivals into enemies. To ensure its safety, like a tyrant who surrounds himself by bodyguards, it invests enormous resources in its own defenses.

9.85 Those who have the chance to live in a community but through their own choice assume the position of a despot and begin to act unilaterally against international society, cannot do anything more foolish. They destroy the natural state of cooperation among people and weaken their own security.

9.86 Cooperation within the framework of international society opens up to humanity the possibility of maintaining the existence of diverse cultures and peoples. Although this diversity is today threatened by many violent conflicts and is being replaced by uniformity, it represents a fundamental value for the further development of humanity.

9.9 Our common future as humankind depends on our appreciation of the diversity of cultures and of mutually complementary values, and on their protection.

10 Conclusion—Seven Principles of a Happy Society

10 Politics is the way of the golden mean.

    10.01 The golden mean is a happy society.

    10.02 The golden mean is the balance point between extremes.

    10.03 A happy society is one in which everyone has an opportunity for self-realization, while respecting the self-realization of others.

. . .

10.1 The first golden principle of a happy society is cooperation.

    10.11 Cooperation is the first principle of humanity.

    10.12 The power of cooperation stems from mutual complementarity.

    10.13 Cooperation is based on diversity, mutual respect, and benevolence.

    10.14 Cooperation is associated with a common goal, a common good, and a division of labor.

        10.141 Cooperation is a mutual exchange of services. Within the framework of cooperation, each person and institution in a society performs an appropriate function.

    10.15 While cooperation is the basis of a constructive culture, domination is the basis of a destructive one, leading states to decline and humanity to ruin.

        10.151 Happiness in society does not come from any form of domination that serves some at the cost of the rest, but from the cooperation, common benefit, and mutual respect of all.

    10.1511 Mutual respect is a fundamental condition of a happy society.

    10.1512 Mutual respect among members of society is expressed in their recognition of value in others and in their kindness and politeness.

10.16 The main goals of the state are the cooperation, liberty, prosperity, and security of its citizens.

    10.161 Freedom without cooperation ends in exploitation, and society disintegrates.

10.17 Every social system should be organized for cooperation. Cooperation should be based on those values that can unite people rather than divide them.

10.18 Cooperation requires the ability to compromise and the consent of all groups in society regarding the scope of the general good, which is common to all and which goes beyond their particular interests.

10.19 All humankind can be linked by cooperation in such areas as common security, crime prevention, hygiene and health, environmental protection, dissemination of scientific knowledge, and setting of international ethical and legal norms.

    . . .

10.2 The second golden principle is that everyone should be happy, but not at the expense of others.

10.21 In a happy society, there is no exploitation, oppression, discrimination, or enslavement.

10.22 In a happy society, people can make plans, take action in order to implement them, and enjoy the fruits of their achievements.

10.23 A happy society is a community of diversity, comprising different classes and espousing complementary values of freedom, entrepreneurship, and nobility.

10.24 In a happy society, citizens are lovers of freedom and of their own country.

10.25 From the principle of happiness for all, there derives the principle that in a society there should be many independent private enterprises: large, medium, and small.

10.251 Entrepreneurship is a source of wealth; it gives independence both material and spiritual, and is the best school of independence and freedom.

10.252 A happy society is a community made up of many private owners; it is not one in which citizens are reduced to a hired workforce and industry, trade, and financial services are dominated by large multinational corporations.

10.253 Entrepreneurship in the home country should be defended against foreign competition, especially in areas such as agriculture, transport, small-scale production, and trade.

10.254 State authorities should also protect strategic sectors of the economy, such as energy, transport, banking, the chemical industry, and defense.

10.26 In a happy society there should be free access to capital; all those with sufficient initiative and good business ideas—especially for projects in the field of innovative technologies—should be able to find resources for their implementation.

10.261 In order to stimulate business activity, legal and tax systems should be simple, stable, and friendly to entrepreneurs.

10.27 A happy society is a prosperous community whose common goal is a good life, and where there are no great differences in wealth.

10.271 A society in which a small group of wealthy people are becoming richer, while an increasing number of poor people are getting poorer, is neither a just nor a happy society—in fact it is not even a community, but only an assemblage of people.

10.272 Poverty nurtures corruption, crime, prostitution, and other negative social phenomena, and prevents people from pursuing their initiatives and self-fulfillment.

10.273 The role of the government is, on the one hand, to create conditions for the full physical and intellectual development of all citizens; and on the other hand, to protect them against poverty, exploitation, crime, and corruption, and to provide them with basic medical care.

10.28 In a happy society there must always be noble and steadfast people—a new knighthood that is able to confront parasitic interest groups, corruption, and crime.

10.281 In order to cooperate effectively, noble and steadfast people should organize themselves in associations and organizations.

10.29 A happy society is a society where the place of honor is given to the moral and intellectual elite, and where people appreciate persons of merit, distinguished scientists, and creators of culture.

. . .

10.3 The third principle is virtues of citizens and wisdom of leaders.

10.31 For any success, there must be a group effort and proper leadership.

10.311 Leaders' wisdom and citizens' virtues are basic prerequisites for a happy society.

10.32 In any country, political leadership should comprise persons who represent in themselves the highest intellectual and moral qualities.

10.321 Heads of state should be comprehensively educated and endowed with considerable life experience and many abilities. They should be able to conduct their own conceptual work, as well as to evaluate opinions of expert advisors.

10.322 An additional requirement for state leaders is nobility and a sense of connectedness with their own country.

10.33 Nobility in politics is expressed in a dedication to the common good and an ability to reconcile the interests of different groups.

10.331 The nobility of citizens lies in their civic virtues: diligence, honesty, courage, respect for the law, and, above all, love of freedom and love of one's country.

10.332 The presence of civic virtues is necessary for effective cooperation among citizens and the existence of a strong state.

10.333 When they lack civic virtues, citizens can be easily manipulated, divided, bribed, and enslaved.

10.34 The presence of wisdom and nobility in politics must be ensured by the electoral law, especially with reference to elections for the Senate.

10.341 The Senate, the upper chamber of Parliament, has an important function in the system of government as the representation of a more meritorious, educated, and experienced part of society, which can potentially balance the less experienced and more populist representation in the lower chamber.

10.35 The electoral system should always be so organized as to select from society the best representatives and to serve the common good, not just the interests of political parties.

10.36 Politics is not a profession, and democracy posits a rotation. At all levels of the elective government, people should be in office only for a limited number of terms.

10.37 In a democracy there must be a place for an elite minority—those who are wise, noble, and best prepared to maintain culture and to govern.

10.371 On the strength, size, social acceptance, and participation in government of such an elite of honor and merit, the prosperity of society and the strength of a given state depend.

10.372 Governing the state is an operation too complex to be entrusted to mediocre people; therefore, we should always look for the best.

10.38 Citizens are united in a community by good leadership, an efficient administration, and the common interest, which lies in having a strong and wealthy state.

10.39 The most important obligation of all citizens, and especially of state leaders, is to work for the benefit of their country and to bear responsibility for its fate.

. . .

10.4 The fourth principle is education for knowledge and virtue.

10.41 Education unites in a harmonious whole the physical development of human beings with their mental development, and tradition with innovation.

10.42 Knowledge must, on the one hand, be based on the cultural heritage of the nation and of all humanity; and on the other, be constantly updated, enriched, and modernized.

10.421 The education system should be consistent and stable—that is, based on a guiding idea related to the purpose of education—while at the same time continuously incorporating new content that is relevant to this idea.

10.422 Superficial reforms and too-frequent changes in curricula destabilize the system of education and lower the level of learning. As a result, students usually lose, while the lobbies of textbook publishers gain.

10.43 The purpose of education is to raise an educated and creative individual, who is physically and mentally well developed, ready to cooperate with others, and equipped with a number of virtues.

10.431 Movement is necessary for people's physical development. The natural activity of children and youth must find creative expression in various forms of play, dance, and sport.

10.432 In the process of the mental development, the lesser emphasis should be placed on memorization, and the greater on the awakening of students' creativity and rationality, so that they learn to search for causal and logical relationships and to engage in analysis.

10.433 During the educational process, students should develop virtues related to cooperation—companionship, civic courage, benevolence, and sociability—as well as acquire sensitivity to social issues and a passion for teamwork.

10.434 Children and adolescents should also be assisted in developing good taste and a personal culture, and in awakening their personal talents and creative predispositions.

10.44 There is a need for a special state-supported organization, such as scouting, that can cooperate with the school and develop in students physical fortitude, self-reliance, courage, and other virtues, along with love of their country.

10.45 A proper relationship between teacher and student is necessary for success in instruction. Teachers must first of all be friends. They must recognize talents and values in their students and give them strength and encouragement, and should reward rather than punish them.

10.46 The learning evaluation system should be neither too strict nor too lenient.

10.461 A system of education that is too strict and condemns the majority of students to receive low scores is unreasonable and harmful. It leads students to acquire a sense that they are themselves of low value. This feeling gives rise to cynicism, prostitution, and aggression.

10.47 The abundance of life-developing forces, the impetus that sometimes manifests in adolescents as aggression, should be used and directed to a positive expression: to action, work, and creativity.

10.48 Everyone, regardless of financial status and social background, should have equal access to knowledge and education.

10.49 Citizens who are educated and creative, who cooperate with one another, who love their country and are at the same time willing to serve all humankind, are the greatest assets of any nation.

. . .

10.5　The fifth principle is good laws.

10.51　The essence of law is justice.

10.52　Natural law, based on right reason and our moral sense, is a measure of the positive laws promulgated by the authorities.

10.53　Good laws serve the common good of the whole society, and not the particular interests of any pressure groups.

10.54　Good law must be based on the understanding of what is right and proper; in the final instance, it always refers to the highest values of human life.

10.55　There is a relationship between law and ethics. Law is a school of morality. Laws perpetuate certain customs, and because of them people take on certain characteristics.

10.551　The primary goal of every legislator is conscious legislative activity whose purpose is the ennoblement of society.

10.552　To direct people toward the good, laws must nurture habits that produce virtues in them and are based on traditional norms of behavior in their society.

10.56　A positive law cannot be arbitrary, but should always be based on the historical experience and traditions of a country.

10.561　If positive laws are made without reference to the traditions and customs existing in a society, they can be perceived as immoral and will be obeyed only under coercion. Then, respect for authority and the force of law will both decrease.

10.562　If a vicious action becomes an accepted practice by force of law, then a sense of the immorality of this action gradually vanishes, and the society undergoes demoralization.

10.57 If the laws and institutions in a country are to fulfill their roles effectively, they must be subject to evolution. However, before the old law, which for a long time was considered right, is to be changed, one needs to prove that the establishment of the new law will bring about a substantial benefit for the entire political community.

10.58 Law is based on sanctions that have the character of external coercion. With moral progress in society, as people internalize morality, learn to act uprightly and gain respect for the law, sanctions can be eased.

    10.581 Sanctions should lead to the desired effect, which is the enforcement of obedience to the law, and should be neither too punitive nor too lax.

    10.582 Corruption among judges and prosecutors results in the degradation of the social order and is a serious crime; therefore, it deserves the highest punishment.

    10.583 Fighting corruption in the judiciary and the police is one of the most important tasks of the state. In order to combat such corruption, special units should be established.

10.59 Good laws and good institutions are necessary conditions of the good state and a happy society. When the law is sloppy and the judiciary and other state institutions are corrupt, citizens lose their integrity and society becomes demoralized.

. . .

10.6 The sixth principle is political knowledge.

    10.61 A happy society needs reliable knowledge concerning politics.

    10.62 Without reliable political knowledge, people can be easily manipulated and indoctrinated.

    10.63 The media should provide true information about current events in the country and the world, and reliable political analyses conducted from different perspectives; they should not limit their coverage to selective reports, biased analyses, politicians' quarrels, and chronicles of accidents.

10.64 In politics we should be neither naïve nor cynical.

    10.641 To be naïve means to be blind to the selfishness by which individuals, political parties, political pressure groups, multinational corporations, and states are so often driven in politics, and to underrate the importance of power in international relations.

    10.642 To be cynical means to reject ethical principles and the possibility of cooperation among human beings, and to think of politics only in terms of power and the struggle for power.

10.65 The art of governing consists of balancing the interests of different groups, classes, and institutions within a society, and of protecting that society against internal and external threats.

10.66 The state serves all citizens and defends society against military conquest, economic dependence, and cultural enslavement.

    10.661 The primary task of any country is to protect its political independence, cultural heritage, and material wealth.

10.67 The security of the state is enhanced by good laws and a good army based on a draft.

    10.671 Good laws and good troops contribute to social discipline, and discipline is needed in any effective organization.

10.68 Foreign policy should be rational and pragmatic: avoiding moralism and ideology, based on a clearly defined national interest, seeking common interests with other states, and contributing to the building of a strong international society made up of independent states.

10.69 A good state has great value. The role of the state as the defender of society is especially important in the era of globalization.

. . .

10.7 The seventh principle of a happy society is the continuity of generations.

    10.71 Traditions, religions, and ancestral memory uphold people in a community.

    10.72 A common culture and a common identity are foundations of any happy society.

    10.73 A strong state is based on the relationships among different social groups that work together because of their common language, traditions, customs, and values.

        10.731 When the civic virtues and bonds that connect people in a community are destroyed, only individuals' own selfishness remains—a selfishness that leads society to demoralization and the state to collapse.

    10.74 The basis for the coexistence of many cultures in one country is nativeculturalism, or the dominant position of the native culture—the culture on which the state was founded and to which it owes its development.

        10.741 The dominance of the native culture is coupled with a tolerance for other cultures.

    10.75 Societies owe their continued survival to the existence of the primary institution of humankind: the family, which begins with marriage between a man and a woman, and is established for the sake of having children.

        10.751 Parentsexuality is a privileged form of sexuality.

    10.76 The family enjoys special protection against poverty and has autonomy.

        10.761 Any interference by the state in the internal affairs of the family should be kept to a minimum.

    10.77 There is no one perfect model of the civilizational development of humanity, nor any one society that can be a perfect model for all others. The differentiation of humankind into nations—independent cultural entities that learn from one another—is the basis of civilizational progress and of human evolution.

10.78 Evolutionity replaces modernity and postmodernity. In this new evolutionary age, we should create novelty on the basis of our traditions and positive values, and while recognizing the contribution of religions to the evolution of humankind, seek to uncover what is truly valuable in them—their spirituality.

10.79 Human beings live by the light of a transcendental perspective whose ultimate purpose is to know God. The basis of a happy society is religious tolerance. The existence of a multitude of ways to know God should be guaranteed in every country.

. . .

10.8 Revolutions usually lead us to disappointments. There is nothing in culture that can be built completely anew. Progress occurs not only because of new ideas, but also because of our better understanding and use of old resources.

10.9 The vigor of ideas depends on their continual renewal in novel forms, and not in their continuity without change.

11 Final Words

11 These are three words that form a whole: life, freedom, and cooperation.

11.1 The purpose of the evolution of life is its fullness and perfection. Human evolution is a journey to ever-greater freedom, and moral and intellectual perfection.

Bibliography

The following select bibliography provides information on sources that have been either referred to or otherwise used in the present work.

Amiel, Henri-Frédéric. *Amiel's Journal*. Trans. Humphrey Ward, Lenox, MA: Hard Press, 2006.

Aquinas, Saint Thomas. *Political Writings*. Ed. and trans. R. W. Dyson. Cambridge: Cambridge UP, 2002.

Aristotle. *Nicomachean Ethics*. Trans. Terence Irwin. 2nd ed. Indianapolis: Hackett, 1999.

Aristotle. *Politics*. Trans. C.D.C. Reeve. Indianapolis: Hackett, 1998.

Becker, Theodore L. (Ed.). *Quantum politics: Applying Quantum Theory to Political Phenomena*. New York: Praeger, 1991.

Bloch, Ernst. *Erbschaft dieser Zeit*. Berlin: Suhrkamp, 1985.

Capra, Fritjof. *The Turning Point: Science, Society, and the Rising Culture*. London: Bantam, 1988.

Chardin, Teilhard, de. *The Phenomenon of Man*. New York: Harper, 2008.

Cicero. *On Duties*. Ed. M. T. Griffin and E. M. Atkins. Cambridge: Cambridge UP, 1991.

Confucius. *The New Analects: Confucius Reconstructed*. Ed. Qian Ning. Shanghai: Shanghai Press, 2013.

Coward, Harold. *The Perfectibility of Human Nature in Eastern and Western Thought*. Albany, NY: SUNY 2008.

Farabi, Abu Nasr, Al-. *On the Perfect State*, Trans. R. Waltzer, Chicago: Kazi, 1998.

Fukuyama, Francis. *The End of History and Last Man*. New York: Avon, 2006.

Gamble, Andrew. *An Introduction to Modern Social and Political Thought*. London: Macmillan, 1981.

Grotius, Hugo. *The Rights of War and Peace*. Trans. A. C. Campbell. Westport, VA: Hyperion, 1993.

Hansell, Gregory A. and William Grassie (Eds.). *Humanity Plus Minus. Transhumanism and Its Critics. Philadelphia*: Metanexus, 2011.

Heisenberg, Werner. *Physics and Philosophy: The Revolution in Modern Science*. Introduction by F. S. C. Northrop. New York: Prometheus, 1985.

Hobbes, Thomas. *Leviathan*. Ed. Edwin Curley. Indianapolis: Hackett, 1994.

Hoene-Wroński, Josef M. *Messianisme, Union Finale de La Philosophie Et de La Religion Constituant. La Philosophie Absolue*. Maurepass: Hachette Livre-Bnf, 2013.

Huntington, Samuel P. *Clash of Civilizations and the Remaking of World Order*. New York: Simon & Shuster, 2013.

Huxley, Julian. *Evolutionary Humanism*. New York: Prometheus, 1992.

Jackson, Robert and Georg Sørensen. *Introduction to International Relations: Theories and Approaches*. Oxford: Oxford UP, 2003.

Jung, Hwa Yol. "Postmodernity, Eurocentrism, and the Future of Political Philosophy," in: *Border Crossing: Toward a Comparative Political Theory*. Ed. F. Dallmayr. Lanhman: Lexington, 1999.

Kinney, Ann M. "The Meaning of Dialectic in Plato," *Auslegung: A Journal of Philosophy* 10.3 (1983), 229–246.

Kirk, G.S., J. E. Raven and M. Schofield. *The Presocratic Philosophers*. 2nd ed. Cambridge: Cambridge UP, 1983.

Koneczny, Feliks. *On the Plurality of Civilizations*. London: Polonica, 1962.

Korab-Karpowicz, W. J. *On the History of Political Philosophy*. New York, NY: Routledge, 2016.

Layne, Christopher. "Kant or Cant: The Myth of Democratic Peace," *International Security* 19.2 (1994), 5–49.

Leon, Jeffrey C. *Science and Philosophy in the West*. Upper Saddle River, NJ: Prentice Hall, 1999.

Locke, John. *Second Treatise of Government*. Ed. C. B. Macpherson. Indianapolis: Hackett, 1980.

Machiavelli, Niccolò. *The Discourses*. 2 vols. Trans. Leslie Walker. London: Routledge, 1975.

Machiavelli, Niccolò. *The Prince*. Trans. Harvey C. Mansfield, Jr. Chicago: Chicago UP, 1985.

Malinowski, Bronislaw. *Freedom and Civilization*. New York: Roy, 1944.

Manu. *The Law Code of Manu*. Transl. P. Olivelle. Oxford: Oxford UP, 2009.

Marias, Julian. *History of Philosophy*. Trans. S. Applebaum and C. C. Strowbridge. New York: Dover, 1967.

Maxwell, Nicholas. *The Comprehensibility of the Universe: A New Conception of Science*. Oxford: Clarendon, 1998.

Mill, John Stuart. *On Liberty and Other Essays*. Ed. John Gray. Oxford World Classics. Oxford: Oxford UP, 1998.

Morgenthau, Hans J. *Politics Among Nations: The Struggle for Power and Peace*. 2nd ed. New York: Knopf, 1956.

Morris, Christopher. "State Coercion and Force," *Social Philosophy and Policy* 29.1 (2012), 28–49.

Niebuhr, Reinhold. *The Nature and Destiny of Man*. Vol. 1 and 2. New York: Charles Scriber's Sons, 1964.

Penrose, Roger. *The Road to Reality: A Complete Guide to the Laws of the Universe*. New York: Vintage, 2004.

Pinker, Steven. *The Better Angels of Our Nature: Why Violence Has Declined*. New York: Penguin, 2011.

Plato. *Republic*. Trans. G. M. A. Grube (revised by C.D.C. Reeve). Indianapolis: Hackett, 1992.

Ramamurty, A. (Aryasamayajula), *Vedanta and Its Philosophical Development*. New Delhi: D. K. Printworld, 2006.

Rousseau, Jean-Jacques. *On the Social Contract*. Trans. G. D. H. Cole. New York: Dover, 2003.

Rumi, Jalal Al-Din. *The Essential Rumi*. Trans. C. Barks. New York: Harper, 1995.

Schmitt, Carl. *The Concept of the Political*. Trans. G. Schwab. Chicago: Chicago UP, 2007.

Thucydides. *On Justice, Power, and Human Nature: The Essence of Thucydides' History of the Peloponnesian War*. Ed. and trans. Paul Woodruff. Indianapolis: Hackett, 1993.

Vogelin, Eric. *The World of the Polis*. Baton Rouge: Louisiana State UP, 1957.

Waltz, Kenneth. *Theory of International Politics*. Reading, MA: Addison-Wesley, 1979

Walzer, Michael. *Just and Unjust Wars: A Moral Argument With Historical Illustrations*. New York: Basic Books, 1977.

Weber, Max. *Politics as Vocation*. Trans. H. H. Gerth, and C. W. Mills. New York: Free Press, 1946.

Wendt, Alexander. *Quantum Mind and Social Science: Unifying Physical and Social Ontology*. Cambridge: Cambridge UP, 2015.

Wendt, Alexander. *Social Theory in International Relations*. Cambridge: Cambridge UP, 1999.

Witkiewicz, Stanislaw I. *O idealizmie i realizmie. Pojęcia i twierdzenia implikowane przez pojęcie istnienia.* Warszawa: PWN, 1977.

Wittgenstein, Ludwig. *Tractatus Logico-Philosophicus*. (English/German Edition) Transl. C. K. Ogden. Oxford: Routledge, 1922.

Zohar, Danah. *The Quantum Self: Human Nature and Consciousness Defined by the New Physics*. New York: Morrow, 1990.

Index

The **bold** entries refer to definitions of words.